PHONICS

SPECTRUM

Columbus, Ohio

Index of Skills

Phonics Grade 2

Numerals indicate the exercise pages on which these skills appear.

Auditory Skills

Associate sounds with letters—*all activities*

Discriminate consonant sounds—40, 41, 42, 43, 44, 45, 67, 70, 71, 72, 73, 74, 76

Discriminate initial sounds—6, 7, 46, 47, 48, 49, 50, 51, 52, 62, 63, 64, 65, 66, 67, 68, 69, 99, 100, 103, 104

Discriminate final sounds—6, 7, 53, 54, 55, 56, 57, 58, 59, 60, 61, 101, 102, 103, 104

Discriminate vowel sounds—8, 9, 10, 11, 12, 13, 14, 15, 16, 17, 18, 19, 20, 21, 22, 23, 24, 25, 26, 27, 28, 29, 30, 31, 32, 33, 34, 35, 36, 37, 38, 39, 77, 78, 79, 80, 81, 82, 83, 84, 85, 86, 87, 88, 89, 90, 91, 92, 93, 94, 95, 96, 97, 98, 105, 106, 107, 108, 109, 110, 111, 112, 113, 114, 115, 116, 117, 118, 119, 120, 121

Following directions—*all activities*

Recognize rhyming words—12, 16, 18, 21, 31, 33, 53, 56, 59, 77, 87, 89, 102, 110, 120

Visual Skills

Discriminate pictures/identify objects—*all activities*

Discriminate words—9, 10, 11, 12, 13, 14, 15, 17, 19, 20, 22, 24, 26, 27, 28, 29, 30, 32, 34, 35, 39, 40, 41, 42, 43, 45, 47, 49, 51, 52, 55, 57, 58, 60, 61, 63, 64, 65, 68, 69, 70, 72, 73, 74, 76, 78, 79, 80, 82, 83, 85, 88, 89, 90, 91, 92, 93, 94, 95, 96, 97, 100, 103, 104, 105, 107, 109, 111, 112, 113, 114, 116, 117, 119

Writing Skills

Write letters—6, 7, 23, 25, 27, 29, 31, 33, 37, 44, 46, 48, 50, 53, 56, 59, 62, 66, 67, 86, 99, 101, 106, 108, 115, 118

Write words—9, 10, 11, 12, 13, 14, 15, 16, 17, 18, 19, 20, 21, 22, 24, 25, 26, 27, 28, 29, 30, 31, 32, 33, 34, 35, 36, 38, 39, 40, 41, 42, 43, 45, 47, 49, 51, 52, 53, 55, 56, 58, 59, 61, 64, 65, 68, 69, 70, 72, 73, 74, 76, 77, 78, 79, 80, 82, 83, 85, 86, 87, 88, 89, 90, 91, 92, 94, 95, 96, 97, 98, 99, 100, 101, 102, 103, 104, 105, 107, 109, 110, 111, 112, 114, 115, 116, 117, 118, 119, 120, 121

Write sentences—13, 15, 19, 26, 47, 49, 51, 60, 63, 67, 68, 71, 73, 75, 80, 81, 83, 84, 92, 109, 113, 114

Short Vowels

a—8, 9, 10, 23, 35, 36, 37, 38

e—11, 12, 13, 23, 35, 36, 37, 38

i—14, 15, 16, 23, 35, 36, 37, 38

o—17, 18, 19, 23, 35, 36, 37, 38

u—20, 21, 22, 23, 35, 36, 37, 38

Long Vowels

a—25, 26, 33, 34, 35, 36, 37, 38, 77, 78, 79

e—80, 81, 82

i—27, 28, 33, 34, 35, 36, 37, 38

o—29, 30, 33, 34, 35, 36, 37, 38, 83, 84, 85

u—31, 32, 33, 34, 35, 36, 37, 38

y—95, 96, 97

Other Vowel Sounds

ar—105, 106, 110, 111, 112, 113

au—89, 90, 91, 94

aw—89, 90, 91, 94

er—105, 106 , 111, 112

ew—92, 93, 94

ir—107, 108, 110, 111, 112, 113

oi—114, 115, 116, 120, 121

oo—87, 88, 94

or—107, 108, 110, 111, 112, 113

ou—117, 118, 119, 120, 121

ow—117, 118, 119, 120, 121

oy—114, 115, 116, 120, 121

ur—109, 110, 111, 112, 113

Consonant Blends—46, 47, 48, 49, 50, 51, 52, 53, 54, 55, 56, 57, 58, 59, 60, 61, 62, 63, 64, 65, 66

Consonant Pairs—99, 100, 101, 102, 103, 104

Silent Consonants—67, 68, 69, 70, 71, 72, 73, 74, 75, 76

Table of Contents

School Specialty
Publishing

Text Copyright © 2007 School Specialty Publishing. Published by Spectrum, an imprint of School Specialty Publishing, a member of the School Specialty Family.
Art Copyright © 2001 Mercer Mayer.

A Big Tuna Trading Company, LLC/J.R. Sansevere Book

Send all inquiries to: School Specialty Publishing, 8720 Orion Place, Columbus OH 43240-2111

ISBN 0-7696-8072-0

2 3 4 5 6 7 8 9 10 WAL 10 09 08 07

Name _____

Review: Beginning and Ending Sounds

Directions: Say the name of each picture. Write the missing letter or letters to complete each word.

ta_g_

___an

_B_u_s_

_m_op

si_x_

_s_u_n_

_w_eb

_ha_t_

Name _____

Review: Beginning and Ending Sounds

Directions: Say the name of each picture. Write the missing letter or letters to complete each word.

_C_an

_m_a_p_

do_g_

_p_ig

_t_op

be_d_

_f_an

_h_a_m_

Short a

Directions: Connect all the pictures whose names have the short **a** sound from the cat to the bag.

Short a

Directions: Write the word from the Word Box that names each picture.

van	cab	cap	apple	map	pan
add	ham	ant	can	hand	ax

cab

ant

van

apple

map

pan

hand

1 + 1 = 2

add

can

ham

cap

ax

Short a

Directions: Write the word from the Word Box that best completes each sentence.

| pan | hand | hat | has | ant | as | ham | apple | am |

1. An ___apple___ is very tiny.

2. Can you ___hand___ Dad the bag?

3. I wear a ___hat___ .

4. I ___am___ glad.

5. He is ___as___ tall as a yardstick.

6. Mom will fry fish in a ___pan___ .

7. We had ___ham___ for lunch.

8. She ___has___ a new hat.

9. The ___ant___ is red.

Short e

Directions: Write the word from the Word Box that names each picture.

| desk | bed | net | tent | web | leg |
| nest | hen | egg | jet | belt | dress |

bed

egg

net

leg

hen

jet

belt

tent

desk

web

dress

nest

Short e

Directions: Write a word that rhymes with each word below.

1. nest _____

2. net _____

3. jet _____

4. sled _____

5. hen _____

Directions: Draw a picture of something whose name has the short **e** sound. Then, write the word that names the picture.

_____

Short e

Directions: Write the word from the Word Box that best completes each sentence.

beg	smell	net	wet	nest

1. Dad had the frog in a _____.

2. The bird sleeps in its _____.

3. Can you _____ the flower?

4. The shirt is _____.

5. My dog likes to _____.

Directions: Write two short **e** words of your own. Then, use each word in a sentence.

1. _____   2. _____

1. _____

_____

2. _____

_____

Short i

Directions: Write the word from the Word Box that names each picture.

hill	dig	fish	bib	sit
milk	hit	ring	six	sip

1.

2.

3.

4.

5.

6.

7.

8.

9.

10.

Short i

Directions: Write the word from the Word Box that best completes each sentence.

lid	zip	dig	milk	crib

1. Blue likes to _____ in the yard.

2. Mom put the baby in the _____.

3. We drink _____ at lunch.

4. Gabby put the _____ on the pan.

5. I can _____ my coat.

Directions: Draw a picture of something whose name has the short **i** sound. Then, write a sentence that tells about your picture.

_____

_____

Short i

Directions: Draw a picture of something that rhymes with each word below. Then, write the rhyming word.

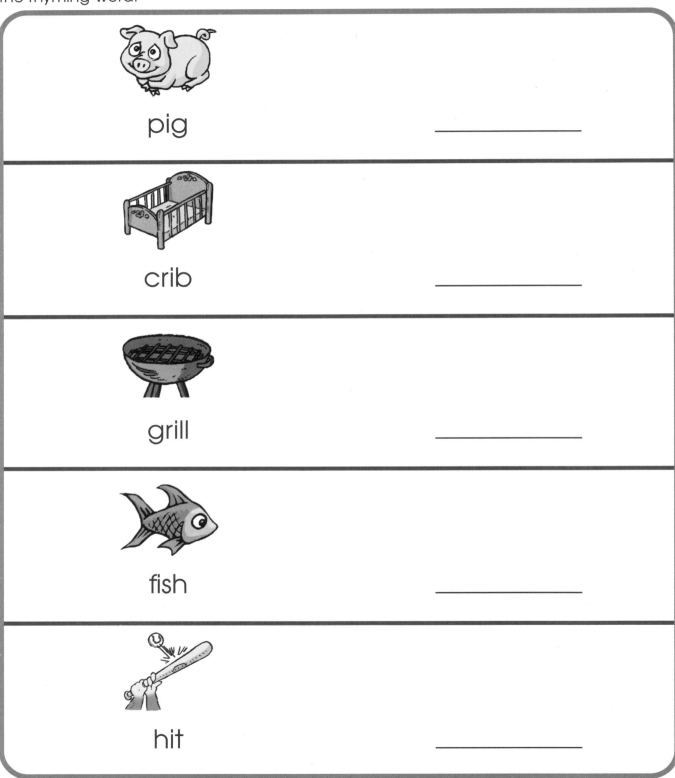

pig _____

crib _____

grill _____

fish _____

hit _____

Short o

Directions: Write the word from the Word Box that names each picture.

dots ✓	cot ✓	lock ✓	cob ✓	box ✓	doll ✓
rod ✓	top ✓	pot ✓	hop ✓	fox ✓	mop ✓

cot

rod

doll

pot

fox

lock

dots

box

mop

hop

top

cob

Short o

Directions: Draw a picture of something that rhymes with each word below. Then, write the rhyming word.

box _____

mop _____

lock _____

spot _____

frog _____

Short o

Directions: Write the word from the Word Box that best completes each sentence.

hop	top	cot	hot	chop

1. Molly sleeps on the _____.

2. Dad can _____ with the ax.

3. The pot is very _____.

4. The bunny likes to _____.

5. Can you spin a _____?

Directions: Draw a picture of something whose name has the short **o** sound. Then, write a sentence that tells about your picture.

_____

_____

Short u

Directions: Write the word from the Word Box that names each picture.

run	cub	pup	tub	nuts	sun
bus	mug	hug	bug	bun	rug

_____ _____ _____

_____ _____ _____

_____ _____ _____

_____ _____ _____

Short u

Directions: Draw a picture of something that rhymes with each word below. Then, write the rhyming word.

bun   _____

jump   _____

hug   _____

cub   _____

pup   _____

Short u

Directions: Write the word from the Word Box that best completes each sentence.

| bus | drum | sun | rug | bug |

1. The _____ is very hot.

2. I take the _____ to school.

3. I see a _____ on my leg.

4. The _____ is green and blue.

5. I can play the _____.

Directions: Draw a picture of something whose name has the short **u** sound. Then, write the word that names the picture.

_____

Name _____

Review: Short Vowels

Directions: Write a vowel in the middle of each puzzle that will make a word across and down.

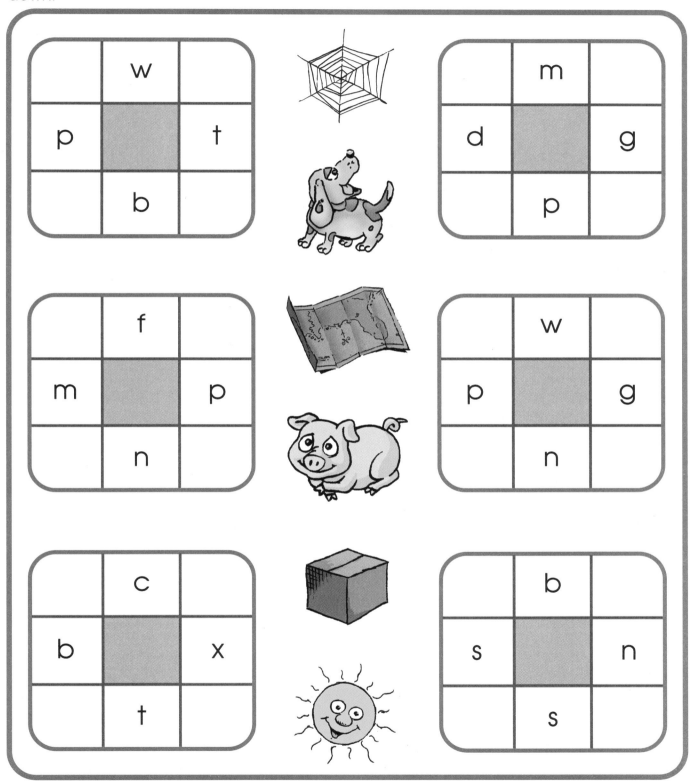

Check Up: Short Vowels

Directions: Write the word from the Word Box that names each picture.

| fox | jump | tag | bed | cup | six | top | map |

Directions: Write a word that has each short vowel sound listed below. Use different words than those above.

1. **a** _____

2. **e** _____

3. **i** _____

4. **o** _____

5. **u** _____

Long a

Directions: Circle each picture that has the long **a** sound.

Directions: Fill in the missing letters **a** and **e** for each word. Then, write each word again.

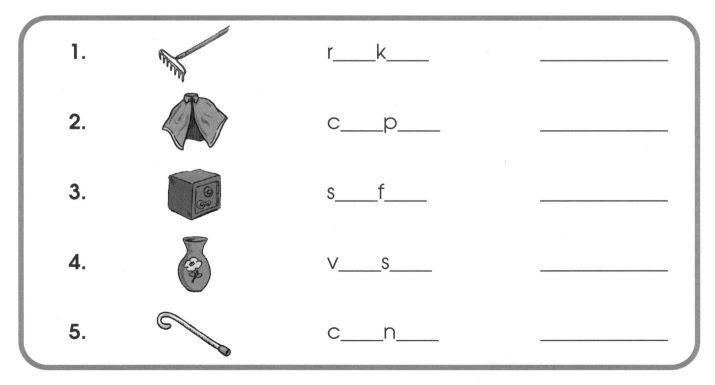

1. r____k____   _____

2. c____p____   _____

3. s____f____   _____

4. v____s____   _____

5. c____n____   _____

Long a

Directions: Draw a picture of something that has the long **a** sound. Then, write a sentence that tells about your picture.

_____

_____

Directions: Write the word from the Word Box that best completes each sentence.

ape	lake	cane	vase	bake	game

1. We swim in the _____.

2. Mom put flowers in the _____.

3. Little Sister plays a _____.

4. I will _____ a cake.

5. Grandpa needs a _____ to walk.

6. We saw an _____ at the zoo.

Long i

Directions: Draw a line to match each picture with its name.

| bite | slide | line | hive | pine |

Directions: Write the missing letters **i** and **e** for each word. Then, write each word again.

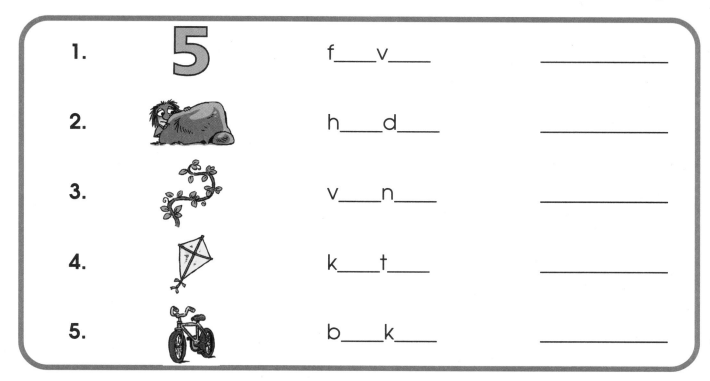

1. f___v___ _____

2. h___d___ _____

3. v___n___ _____

4. k___t___ _____

5. b___k___ _____

Long i

Directions: Draw a picture of something that has the long **i** sound. Then, write the word that names the picture.

_____

Directions: Write the word from the Word Box that best completes each sentence.

bite	dive	kite	ride	bike	pine

1. My _____ is up in the tree.

2. I ride my _____ to school.

3. I like the smell of _____ trees.

4. Can you _____ a horse?

5. Take a _____ of the apple.

6. Little Critter will _____ into the lake.

Long o

Directions: Write the word from the Word Box that names each picture.

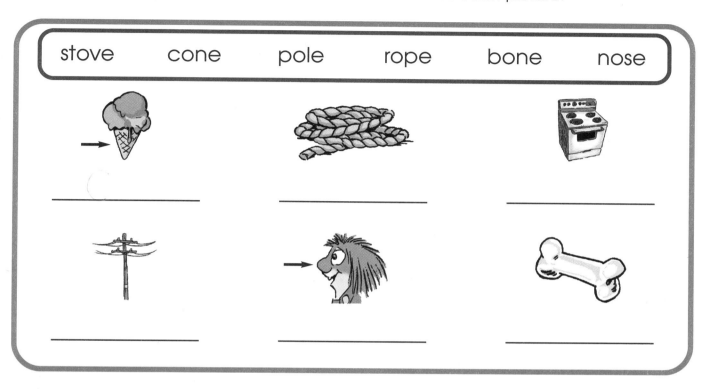

| stove | cone | pole | rope | bone | nose |

_____   _____   _____

_____   _____   _____

Directions: Write the missing letters **o** and **e** for each word. Then, write each word again.

1.   r__o__s__e__   _____

2.   st__o__n__e__   _____

3.   h__o__s__e__   _____

Long o

Directions: Write the word from the Word Box that best completes each sentence.

hose	note	rose	stove	rope	bone

1. Mom gave Dad a _____.

2. Put the _____ in the car.

3. Little Critter will give Blue a _____.

4. Can you sing that _____?

5. Dad has a green _____ in the yard.

6. The _____ is very hot.

Directions: Write the word that names each picture below.

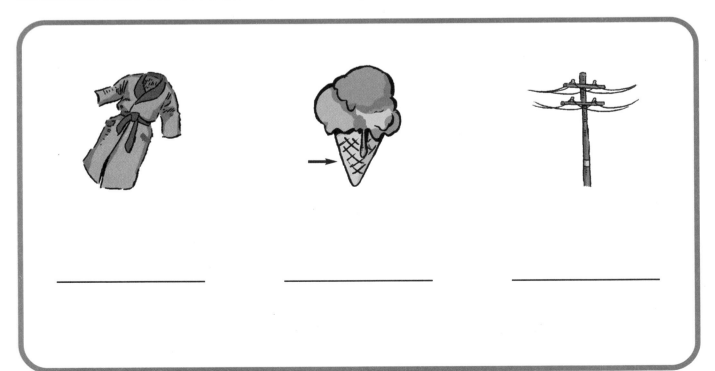

_____   _____   _____

Long u

Directions: Write the missing letters **u** and **e** for each word. Then, write each word again.

1.   t___n___   _____

2.   m___l___   _____

3.    d___n___   _____

4.   c___t___   _____

5.   c___b___   _____

Directions: Write a word that rhymes with each word below.

1.    tube   _rub_

2.   prune   _run_

3.   flute   _lute_

Long u

Directions: Circle the word that names the picture. Then, write the word on the line.

cub
cube
cup

_____

rug
mule
ruler

_____

mug
mule
tune

_____

cute
flute
fun

_____

tune
nut
tube

_____

den
dune
tune

_____

dune
tune
prune

_____

tub
tuba
tube

_____

cute
cut
cube

_____

Review: Long Vowels

Directions: Write the missing vowels to complete each word.

1.   r___k___

2.   r___b___

3.   t___p___

4.   t___b___

5.   k___t___

Directions: Write a word that rhymes with each word below.

1. vine   _____   5. wave   _____

2. gate   _____   6. like   _____

3. hose   _____   7. tune   _____

4. cube   _____   8. game   _____

Check Up: Long Vowels

Directions: Write the word from the Word Box that names each picture.

| cape | safe | bike | vase | mule | bone |
| hide | prune | hose | cone | cube | nine |

_____   _____   _____

_____   _____   _____

_____   _____   _____

_____   _____   _____

Short and Long Vowels

Directions: Write the word from the Word Box that names each picture.

duck	pan	rod	skate	lips	tape
cub	dress	slide	cone	vine	flute

_____   _____   _____

_____   _____   _____

_____   _____   _____

_____   _____   _____

Short and Long Vowels

Directions: Write each picture name in the correct column.

Short Vowel Words   **Long Vowel Words**

_____   _____

_____   _____

_____   _____

_____   _____

_____   _____

Short and Long Vowels

Directions: Write the missing vowel or vowels for each word.

1.   b____g

2.   b____k____

3.    r____p____

4.   b____d

5.    n____s____

6.   t____p

7.   m____p

8.   m____l____

9.   b____b

10.    p____n____

Short and Long Vowels

Directions: Draw a picture of something whose name has the vowel sound written in each box. Then, write the word that names each picture.

Long u	Short a	Short e
_____	_____	_____

Long i	Long o	Short i
_____	_____	_____

Short u	Long a	Short o
_____	_____	_____

Check Up: Short and Long Vowels

Directions: Circle the word that best completes each sentence. Then, write the word in the blank.

1. Little Critter put the hat in the _____.

   bone   box   robe

2. A _____ is a very large animal.

   hag   hose   hog

3. The mother bear takes care of her _____.

   cube   cup   cub

4. Let's play a _____.

   gum   gate   game

5. I will play a _____ on the flute.

   tub   tube   tune

6. Put the _____ on the boat.

   robe   rope   nine

7. I like to go down the _____.

   five   fish   slide

8. He will wash the dog in the _____.

   tub   tube   tag

Name _____

Hard and Soft c

Directions: Draw a line to match each word with its picture.

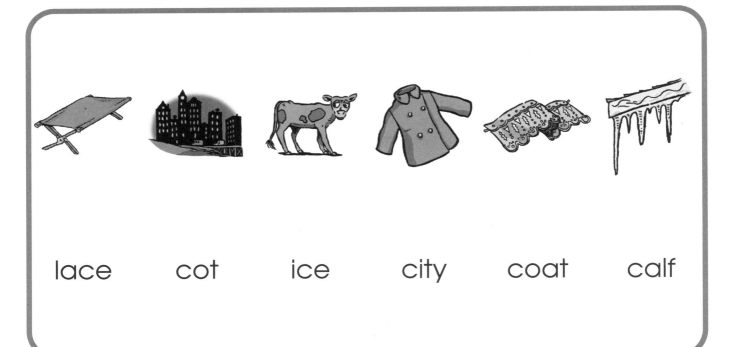

lace   cot   ice   city   coat   calf

Directions: Write each picture name from above in the correct column.

Hard c Words	Soft c Words
_____	_____
_____	_____
_____	_____

Hard and Soft c

Directions: Write the word from the Word Box that names each picture.

pencil	lace	fence	cow	ice	mice
car	cup	cent	cab	face	cap

_____

_____

_____

_____

_____

_____

_____

_____

_____

_____

_____

_____

Hard and Soft g

Directions: Draw a line to match each word with its picture.

cage   stage   garden   game   bridge   gas

Directions: Write each picture name from above in the correct column.

Hard g Words	Soft g Words
_____	_____
_____	_____
_____	_____

Hard and Soft g

Directions: Write the word from the Word Box that names each picture.

| wig | edge | judge | goat | gate | cage |
| stage | hinge | dog | page | bridge | pig |

_____

_____

_____

_____

_____

_____

_____

_____

_____

_____

_____

_____

Name _____

Review: Hard and Soft c and g

Directions: Write the missing letter **c** or **g** for each word. Then, circle the word *hard* or *soft* to tell how the letter sounds.

1. ____as   hard   soft

2. sta____e   hard   soft

3. ____age   hard   soft

4. fa____e   hard   soft

5. i____e   hard   soft

6. brid____e   hard   soft

7. ____alf   hard   soft

8. ____arden   hard   soft

9. jud____e   hard   soft

10. mi____e   hard   soft

Check Up: Hard and Soft c and g

Directions: Circle the word that best completes each sentence. Then, write the word in the blank.

1. Mom has on a _____ dress.

   leg   lace   place

2. We will drive across the _____.

   judge   fence   bridge

3. We saw a _____ at the farm.

   goat   gas   edge

4. Dad goes to work in the _____.

   ice   fence   city

5. Little Critter wears a _____ when it is cold.

   cow   cab   coat

6. What do you plant in your _____?

   cup   cage   garden

7. Mom does not like _____.

   edge   mice   pencil

8. The _____ is a kind man.

   judge   page   cent

Consonant Blends With S

Directions: Write the consonant blend that shows the beginning sound of each picture name.

sn	sk	st	sm	sl	sw

____ake

____one

____ates

____ide

____eps

____oke

____ing

____ile

____ail

____unk

____age

____eep

Consonant Blends With S

Directions: Write the word from the Word Box that names each picture.

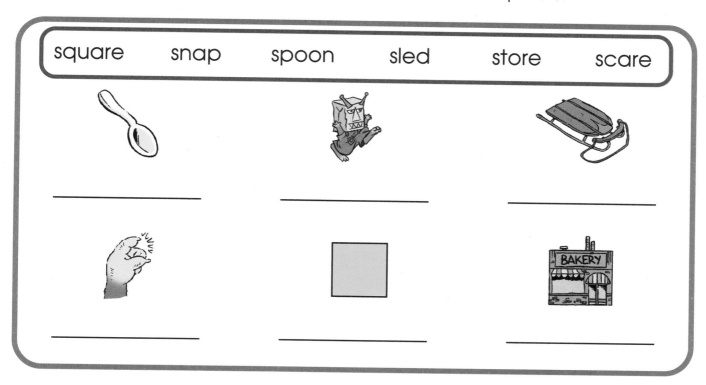

| square | snap | spoon | sled | store | scare |

_____   _____   _____

_____   _____   _____

Directions: Write two sentences. Use one word from above in each sentence.

1. _____

_____

2. _____

_____

Consonant Blends With L

Directions: Write the consonant blend that shows the beginning sound of each picture name.

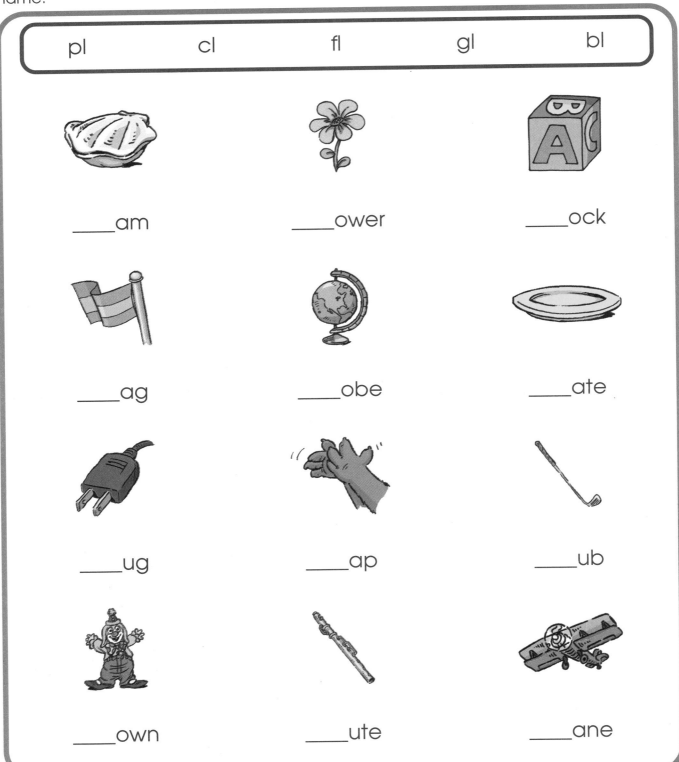

pl   cl   fl   gl   bl

____am   ____ower   ____ock

____ag   ____obe   ____ate

____ug   ____ap   ____ub

____own   ____ute   ____ane

Consonant Blends With L

Directions: Write the word from the Word Box that names each picture.

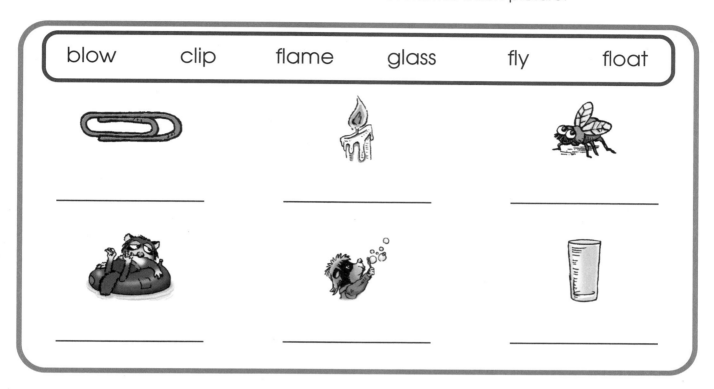

| blow | clip | flame | glass | fly | float |

Directions: Write two sentences. Use one word from above in each sentence.

1. _____

_____

2. _____

_____

Consonant Blends With R

Directions: Write the consonant blend that shows the beginning sound of each picture name.

| dr | br | cr | fr | tr | pr |

___ide

___og

___ow

___idge

___ab

___ess

___um

___ap

___ize

___oom

___ame

___uit

Consonant Blends With R

Directions: Write the word from the Word Box that names each picture.

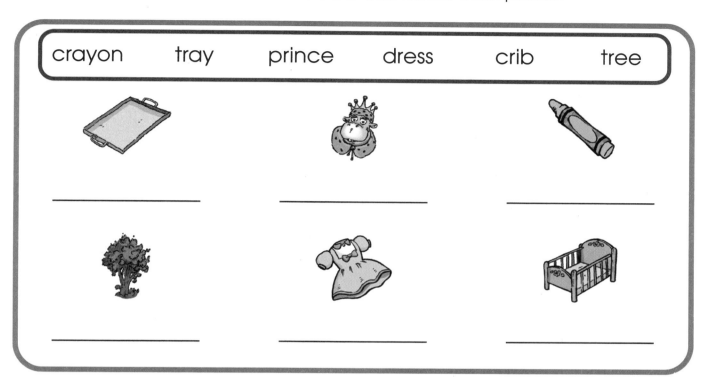

crayon   tray   prince   dress   crib   tree

_____   _____   _____

_____   _____   _____

Directions: Write two sentences. Use one word from above in each sentence.

1. _____

   _____

2. _____

   _____

Review: Consonant Blends

Directions: Write the word from the Word Box that names each picture.

bridge	stage	snake	grass	tree	crab
float	sled	globe	flag	plug	bride

_____

_____

_____

_____

_____

_____

_____

_____

_____

_____

_____

_____

Final Consonant Blends

Directions: Write the final consonant blend for each word. Then, write each word again.

1.   ca_____ _____

2.   de_____ _____

3.   roa_____ _____

4.   toa_____ _____

5.   ma_____ _____

Directions: Write a word that rhymes with each word below.

1.   mist   _____

2.   vest   _____

3.   roast   _____

Final Consonant Blends

Directions: Circle the consonant blend that you hear at the end of each picture name.

st   sk   st   sk   st   sk

st   sk   st   sk   st   sk

st   sk   st   sk   st   sk

st   sk   st   sk   st   sk

Review: Final Consonant Blends

Directions: Write the word from the Word Box that names each picture.

mask	list	vest	desk	fist	mist
chest	tusk	roast	nest	crust	toast

_____ _____ _____

_____ _____ _____

_____ _____ _____

_____ _____ _____

Final Consonant Blends

Directions: Write the final consonant blend of each word. Then, write each word again.

1.   sta_____   _____

2.   pai_____   _____

3.   sku_____   _____

4.   pla_____   _____

5.   ce_____   _____

Directions: Write a word that rhymes with each word below.

1. band   _____

2. stump   _____

3. sink   _____

Name _____

Final Consonant Blends

Directions: Circle the word that names each picture.

pond
point
paint

bank
crank
cent

stand
cent
tent

pump
paint
plant

lamp
pump
stump

wink
sink
wind

band
bank
pond

ant
stand
and

stump
stamp
stand

stump
pond
pump

Review: Final Consonant Blends

Directions: Write the word from the Word Box that names each picture.

cast	cent	mask	hand	plant	lamp
skunk	sink	pond	desk	bank	stamp

_____

_____

_____

_____

Final Consonant Blends

Directions: Write the final consonant blend to complete each word. Then, write each word again.

1. ra_____ _____

2. qui_____ _____

3. wo_____ _____

4. wi_____ _____

5. go_____ _____

Directions: Write a word that rhymes with each word below.

1. shelf _____

2. lift _____

3. melt _____

Final Consonant Blends

Directions: Circle the word that names each picture.

 shelf
elf
wolf

 melt
belt
self

 lift
gift
golf

 left
elf
let

craft
lift
raft

 melt
shelf
elf

Directions: Write two sentences. Use one word that you circled above in each sentence.

1. _____

_____

2. _____

_____

Review: Final Consonant Blends

Directions: Write the word from the Word Box that names each picture.

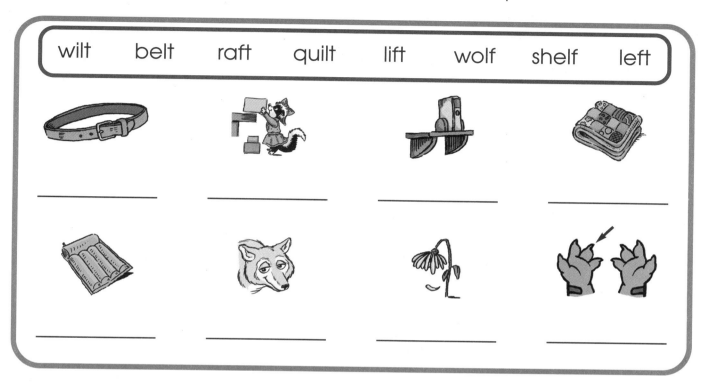

wilt	belt	raft	quilt	lift	wolf	shelf	left

_____   _____   _____   _____

_____   _____   _____   _____

Directions: Look at the picture and write the word that best completes each sentence.

1. The _____ is very small.

2. Mom gave Dad a _____.

3. Do you play _____?

4. Put the books on the _____.

5. The ice will _____ in the sun.

Name _____

Three-Letter Consonant Blends

Directions: Write a three-letter consonant blend to complete each word. Then, write each word again.

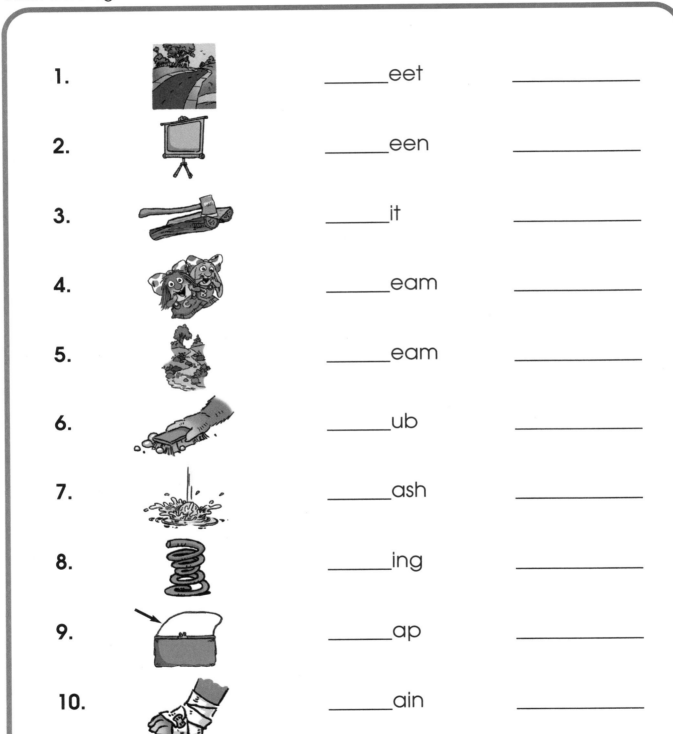

1. _____eet _____

2. _____een _____

3. _____it _____

4. _____eam _____

5. _____eam _____

6. _____ub _____

7. _____ash _____

8. _____ing _____

9. _____ap _____

10. _____ain _____

62   Spectrum Phonics Grade 2

Three-Letter Consonant Blends

Directions: Draw a picture to go with each word below. Then, write a sentence that tells about each picture. Make sure to use the word in the sentence.

scream	street
_____	_____
_____	_____

splash	scrub
_____	_____
_____	_____

Three-Letter Consonant Blends

Directions: Write the word from the Word Box that best completes each sentence.

stripes	scrape	street	sprain	scrub
spray	scrap	splash	stream	

1. There are many houses on my _____.

2. Dad will _____ the garden with the hose.

3. Tiger makes a big _____ when he jumps in the pool.

4. Write your name on this _____ of paper.

5. Grandpa and I fish in the _____.

6. Blue does not like when I _____ him clean.

7. Little Critter has a _____ on his knee.

8. My new kitten has black and gray _____.

9. Mom got a bad _____ when she fell.

Review: 3-Letter Consonant Blends

Directions: Write the word from the Word Box that names each picture.

scream	stripes	scrape	street	strong	scrub
spray	spring	string	split	splash	stream

_____   _____   _____

_____   _____   _____

_____   _____   _____

_____   _____   _____

Check Up: Consonant Blends

Directions: Write a consonant blend to complete each word.

1. ____ing

2. ____ag

3.  ____ay

4.  ____it

5. de____

6. ____own

7. sku____

8.  ne____

9.  ____oon

10.  ____ake

11.  ____idge

12.  ____og

Silent Consonants

Directions: Write the letters **kn** or **wr** to show the beginning sound of each picture name.

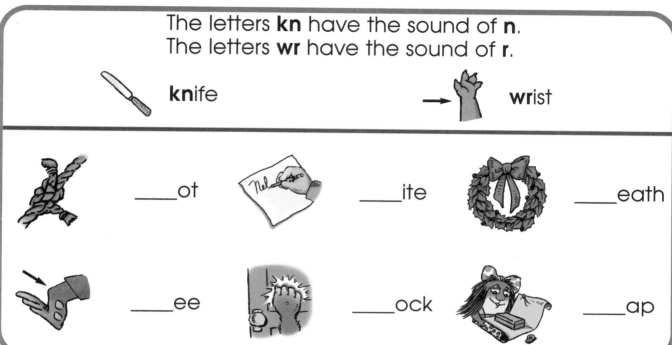

The letters **kn** have the sound of **n**.
The letters **wr** have the sound of **r**.

knife

→ **wr**ist

____ot

____ite

____eath

____ee

____ock

____ap

Directions: Write two sentences. Use one word from above in each sentence.

1. _____

_____

2. _____

_____

Silent Consonants

Directions: Write the word from the Word Box that names each picture.

wrench   knock   wrist   kneel   write   knit

_____   _____   _____

_____   _____   _____

Directions: Write two sentences. Use one word from above in each sentence.

1. _____

   _____

2. _____

   _____

Silent Consonants

Directions: Write the word from the Word Box that best completes each sentence.

knot	write	wrap	knife	
know	knock	knee	knit	wrong

1. Can you _____ this gift for Mom?

2. I _____ how to swim.

3. Gator likes to _____ letters.

4. I fell and hurt my _____.

5. The telephone call was a _____ number.

6. Grandma wants to _____ a scarf for Little Sister.

7. There was a _____ in the rope.

8. I hear a _____at the door.

9. Put a _____ and fork on the table.

Silent Consonants

Directions: Write the word from the Word Box that names each picture.

The letters **ck** have the sound of **k**.

 du**ck**

rock	dock	pocket	brick	
jacket	clock	rocket	tack	truck

_____

_____

_____

_____

_____

_____

_____

_____

_____

Silent Consonants

Directions: Draw a picture to go with each word below. Then, write a sentence that tells about each picture. Make sure to use the word in the sentence.

pocket	rocket
_____ _____	_____ _____
truck	rock
_____ _____	_____ _____

Silent Consonants

Directions: Write the word from the Word Box that best completes each sentence.

pack	duck	snack	chicks	
clock	tricks	lock	black	dock

1. Did you hear that _____ quack?

2. My _____ shows the wrong time.

3. Grandma has baby _____ at the farm.

4. Dad gave me a _____ for my bike.

5. My dog has _____ and white fur.

6. Mom steered the boat to the _____.

7. Little Critter put his books in his _____.

8. Malcolm likes to play _____ on his friends.

9. I am hungry for a _____.

Silent Consonants

Directions: Write the word from the Word Box that names each picture.

When **g** and **h** are together in a word, they are often silent.

 ei**gh**t

| eighty | light | knight | high | bright | night |

 _____

80 _____

 _____

 _____

_____

 _____

Directions: Write two sentences. Use one word from above in each sentence.

1. _____

   _____

2. _____

   _____

Silent Consonants

Directions: Write the word from the Word Box that best completes each sentence.

might	right	fight	night	sight
tight	eighty	light	high	

1. Grandpa is almost _____ years old.

2. We _____ not have school tomorrow.

3. My red jacket is too _____.

4. Mom was _____ about the storm.

5. The snowy trees are a pretty _____.

6. The _____ is very bright.

7. It rained all _____ long.

8. I can't reach that _____ shelf.

9. Dad doesn't like us to _____.

Review: Silent Consonants

Directions: Write a sentence that tells about each picture.

1. _____

2. _____

3. _____

4. _____

5. _____

6. _____

Check Up: Silent Consonants

Directions: Write the word from the Word Box that names each picture.

chick	rock	lock	knit	knight	knock
wrist	write	pocket	wrap	knot	light

_____   _____   _____

_____   _____   _____

_____   _____   _____

_____   _____   _____

Vowel Pairs: AI and AY

Directions: Write a word that rhymes with each word below.

train

_____

tail

_____

tray

_____

clay

_____

snail

_____

Vowel Pairs: AI and AY

Directions: Write the word from the Word Box that names each picture.

clay	pail	tail	train	paint	spray
rain	stain	chain	pay	sail	tray

_____

_____

_____

_____

Vowel Pairs: AI and AY

Directions: Write the word from the Word Box that best completes each sentence.

paint	tray	mail	snail	
rain	tail	clay	train	hay

1. The _____ is in its shell.

2. Dad brought us cookies on a _____.

3. The cows eat _____.

4. Little Critter made a bowl from _____.

5. We don't like to play outside in the _____.

6. Blue wags his _____ when he is happy.

7. What color _____ should we use?

8. Grandma took the _____ when she came to see us.

9. I bring in the _____ every day.

Vowel Pairs: EE and EA

Directions: Write the word from the Word Box that names each picture.

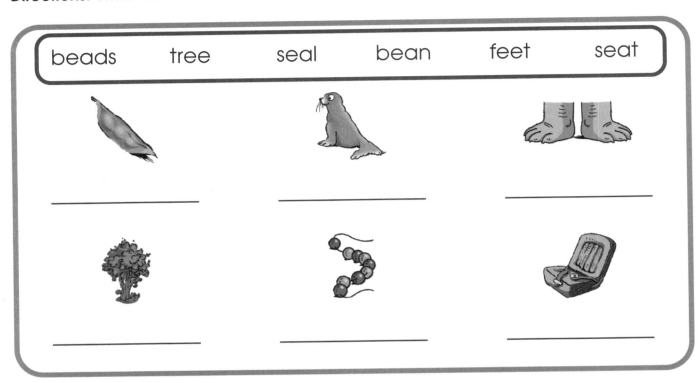

beads	tree	seal	bean	feet	seat

_____   _____   _____

_____   _____   _____

Directions: Write two sentences. Use one word from above in each sentence.

1. _____

_____

2. _____

_____

Vowel Pairs: EE and EA

Directions: Draw a picture to go with each word below. Then, write a sentence that tells about each picture. Make sure to use the word in the sentence.

leaf	bread
_____ _____	_____ _____
feet	sleep
_____ _____	_____ _____

Vowel Pairs: EE and EA

Directions: Write the word from the Word Box that best completes each sentence.

bread	leak	steam	beak	sleep
beach	sheep	head	leap	

1. Our kitchen sink has a _____.

2. Do you like to swim at the _____?

3. The frog can _____ over the log.

4. Mom likes to bake wheat _____.

5. The bird has a very sharp _____.

6. A baby _____ is called a lamb.

7. Little Critter hit his _____ on the shelf.

8. Gator and Tiger will _____ in the tent tonight.

9. I see _____ coming from the teakettle.

Vowel Pairs: OA and OW

Directions: Write the word from the Word Box that names each picture.

| pillow | goat | snow | road | crow | boat |

_____   _____   _____

_____   _____   _____

Directions: Write two sentences. Use one word from above in each sentence.

1. _____

   _____

2. _____

   _____

Vowel Pairs: OA and OW

Directions: Draw a picture to go with each word below. Then, write a sentence that tells about each picture. Make sure to use the word in the sentence.

coat	window
_____	_____
_____	_____

bowl	toad
_____	_____
_____	_____

Vowel Pairs: OA and OW

Directions: Write the word from the Word Box that best completes each sentence.

| toad | row | grown | goat | |
| bowl | throw | toast | coat | pillow |

1. A baby _____ is called a kid.

2. Can you _____ the ball to Tiger?

3. I left my new wool _____ at school.

4. Mom gave me a soft _____.

5. That _____ has bumpy skin.

6. Let's make a _____ of popcorn.

7. The baby has _____ a lot in three months.

8. Dad made eggs and _____ for breakfast.

9. We can _____ the boat into the middle of the lake.

Review: Vowel Pairs

Directions: Write the missing vowel pair for each word. Then, write each word again.

1.  b_e c_k _____

2.  spr_ick aer_ _____

3. s_o u_p _____

4. br_e a_d _____

5. sl_e e_p _____

6. b_o w_l _____

7. s_e a_l _____

8.  sn_e a_l _____

9. l_e a_f _____

10. cr_o w_ _____

Name _____

Vowel Pair: OO

Directions: Write a word that rhymes with each word below.

spoon   *moon*

book   *hook*

spool   *pool*

wood   *hood*

stools   *tools*

Vowel Pair: OO

Directions: Write the word from the Word Box that names each picture.

spoon	boot	moose	hoop	moon	pool
woods	tooth	hood	hoof	broom	book

_____

_____

_____

_____

_____

_____

_____

_____

_____

_____

_____

_____

Vowel Pairs: AU and AW

Directions: In each row, write two words that rhyme with the first word in the row.

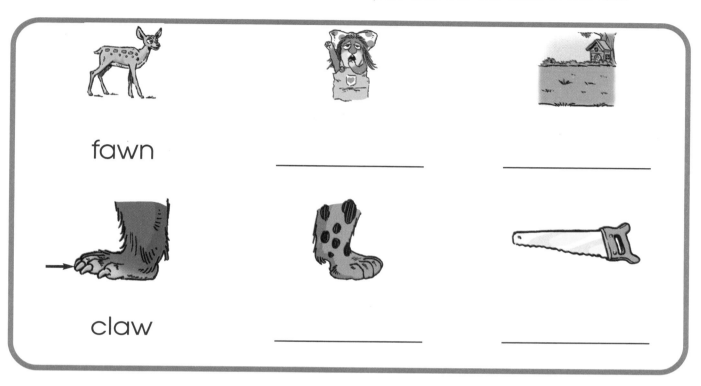

fawn   _____   _____

claw   _____   _____

Directions: Draw lines to match the words and pictures.

sauce   laundry   faucet   auto   caught

Vowel Pairs: AU and AW

Directions: Write the word from the Word Box that names each picture.

straw	shawl	crawl	fawn	auto	claw
caught	sauce	yawn	faucet	laundry	lawn

_____

_____

_____

_____

_____

_____

_____

_____

_____

_____

_____

_____

Vowel Pairs: AU and AW

Directions: Write the word from the Word Box that best completes each sentence.

fawn	caught	straw	auto	
faucet	crawl	shawl	saw	lawn

1. Dad put a new _____ on the sink.

2. A baby deer is called a _____.

3. Mom cut the wood with a _____.

4. My baby brother is just learning to _____.

5. The fish got _____ in the net.

6. Our family bought a new car at the _____ show.

7. The _____ is nice and green in the spring.

8. Grandma wears a _____ to keep warm.

9. Little Critter sips his milk through a _____.

Vowel Pair: EW

Directions: Write the word from the Word Box that names each picture.

news	stew	jewelry	screw

1. _____

2. _____

3.  _____

4. _____

Directions: Write two sentences. Use one word from the Word Box in each sentence.

flew	new	few	grew

1. _____

   _____

2. _____

   _____

Vowel Pair: EW

Directions: Write the word from the Word Box that best completes each sentence.

chew	grew	dew	jewelry	stew
drew	few	flew	news	

1. Last year, we _____ beans in our garden.

2. We went to the beach a _____ times this summer.

3. There is _____ on the lawn in the morning.

4. Have you heard the good _____?

5. Mom made beef _____ for dinner.

6. Little Critter _____ a picture of Mom.

7. Blue likes to _____ on a bone.

8. Little Sister likes to wear _____.

9. The bird _____ high in the sky.

Review: Vowel Pairs

Directions: Write the word from the Word Box that names each picture.

auto	yawn	stew	hood	faucet	fawn
laundry	screw	tooth	claw	book	moose

_____

_____

_____

_____

_____

_____

_____

_____

_____

_____

_____

_____

The Sounds of Y

Directions: Read the words. Write each word in the correct column.

Sometimes **y** can sound like long **e**,
and sometimes it can sound like long **i**.

 puppy    fry

dry   baby   city   sky

pony   fly   bunny   cry

Y as Long e	Y as Long i
_____	_____
_____	_____
_____	_____
_____	_____

The Sounds of Y

Directions: Write the word from the Word Box that names each picture.

spy	fly	cry	penny	muddy	city
puppy	sky	baby	fry	story	dry

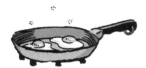

_____ _____ _____

_____ _____ _____

_____ _____ _____

_____ _____ _____

The Sounds of Y

Directions: Write the word from the Word Box that best completes each sentence.

silly   cry   city   story   puppy
try   muddy   happy   fry

1. Can you hear the baby _cry_ ?

2. The _city_ is a busy place.

3. Dad will _try_ not to be late.

4. It is _muddy_ after it rains.

5. Little Critter takes good care of his new _puppy_.

6. Gabby is _happy_ when she reads.

7. Molly will read us a _story_ .

8. Gator told us a _silly_ joke.

9. Do you know how to _fry_ an egg?

Check Up: Vowel Pairs and Sounds of Y

Directions: Write the name of each picture.

_____

_____

_____

_____

_____

_____

_____

_____

_____

_____

_____

_____

_____

_____

_____

Name _____

Consonant Pairs

Directions: Write the letters **sh**, **ch**, **th**, **thr**, or **wh** to complete each word. Then, write each word again.

1. _____op _____

2. _____ead _____

3. _____ell _____

4. _____ee _____

5.  _____ale _____

6. _____ain _____

7. _____in _____

8. _____ick _____

9. _____eel _____

10.  _____oe _____

Consonant Pairs

Directions: Write the word from the Word Box that names each picture.

wheel	ship	chair	whale	shoe	shelf
think	cheese	throat	thread	cheek	thin

_____

_____

_____

_____

_____

_____

_____

_____

_____

_____

_____

_____

Final Consonant Pairs

Directions: Write the consonant pair **sh**, **ch**, **tch**, **th**, or **ng** to complete each word. Then, write each word again.

1. ri____ _____

2. wa____ _____

3.  di____ _____

4.  bran____ _____

5. scra____ _____

6. stri____ _____

7. ba____ _____

8. bru____ _____

9. di____ _____

10. too____ _____

Name _____

Final Consonant Pairs

Directions: Write a word that rhymes with each word below.

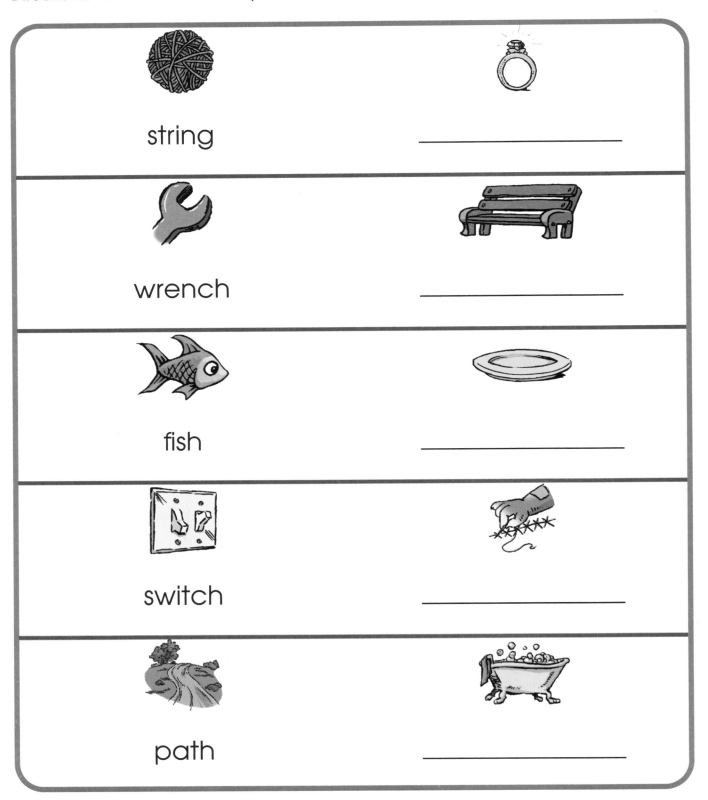

string _____

wrench _____

fish _____

switch _____

path _____

Review: Consonant Pairs

Directions: Write the word from the Word Box that names each picture.

bench	wing	bush	chain	watch	path
three	throne	whale	ship	ring	think

_____   _____   _____

_____   _____   _____

_____   _____   _____

3

_____   _____   _____

Check Up: Consonant Pairs

Directions: Write the word or words from the Word Box that best completes each sentence.

wing	beach	chunk	bring	bench	cheese
shade	wash	path	ship	splash	shoes

1. The mouse ate a _____ of _____.

2. Mom and Dad sailed on a _____.

3. Can you _____ a snack to the picnic?

4. Bun Bun walked on the _____ in the woods.

5. Little Critter is sitting on the green _____ in the park.

6. To stay cool, I sit in the _____.

7. The bluebird has a broken _____.

8. At the _____, we like to _____ in the water.

9. You should _____ your dirty _____.

Vowels With R: AR and ER

Directions: Write the word from the Word Box that names each picture.

jar	barn	yarn	hammer	paper	letter
dart	ladder	slipper	fern	harp	star

_____   _____   _____

_____   _____   _____

_____   _____   _____

_____   _____   _____

Vowels With R: AR and ER

Directions: Write the missing letters **ar** or **er** for each word. Then, write each word again.

1. danc_____ _____

2.  f_____m _____

3.  slipp_____ _____

4.  c_____ _____

5. lett_____ _____

6. y_____n _____

7. p_____k _____

8. camp_____ _____

9.  hamm_____ _____

10. st_____ _____

Vowels With R: IR and OR

Directions: Write the word from the Word Box that names each picture.

dirt	thorn	bird	girl	corn	fort
storm	cork	thirty	fork	shirt	skirt

_____

_____

_____

_____

_____

_____

_____

_____

_____

_____

_____

_____

Vowels With R: IR and OR

Directions: Write the missing letters **ir** or **or** for each word. Then, write each word again.

1. h_____se _____

2. sk_____t _____

3. squ_____t _____

4. st_____m _____

5. g_____l _____

6. c_____n _____

7. sh_____t _____

8. b_____d _____

9.  th_____n _____

10. c_____d _____

Vowels With R: UR

Directions: Write the word from the Word Box that names each picture.

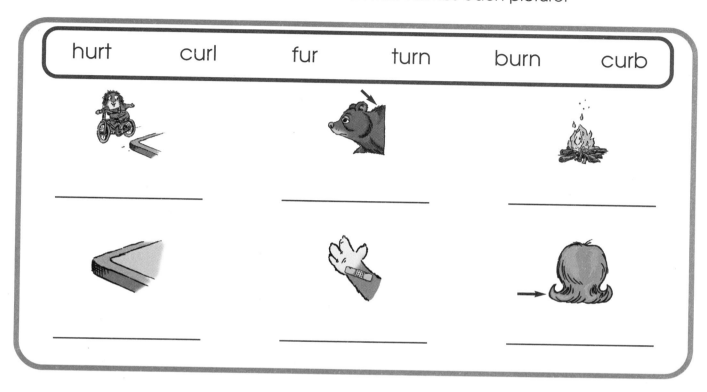

hurt	curl	fur	turn	burn	curb

_____   _____   _____

_____   _____   _____

Directions: Write two sentences. Use one word from above in each sentence.

1. _____

   _____

2. _____

   _____

Vowels With R

Directions: Write a word that rhymes with each word below.

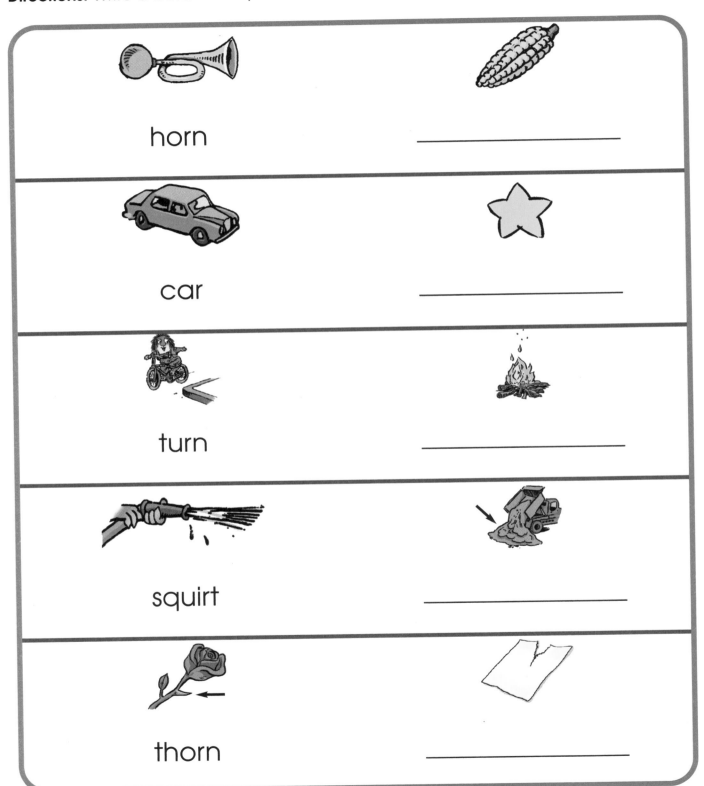

horn

_____

car

_____

turn

_____

squirt

_____

thorn

_____

Vowels With R

Directions: Write the word from the Word Box that best completes each sentence.

| bird | fur | corn | fern | horn |
| cart | barn | hurt | bark | |

1. The bear's _____ keeps it warm.

2. That _____ is a very pretty plant.

3. Little Critter and Grandpa put the hay in the _____.

4. Grandma ate _____ on the cob for dinner.

5. I _____ my foot playing soccer.

6. Blue will _____ when he wants a bone.

7. The _____ has four wheels.

8. Gator found a baby _____ in its nest.

9. Little Sister plays the _____ in the school band.

Review: Vowels With R

Directions: Write the word from the Word Box that names each picture.

| fork | shirt | hurt | bird | star | burn |
| letter | curl | fern | horn | car | barn |

_____   _____   _____

_____   _____   _____

_____   _____   _____

_____   _____   _____

Check Up: Vowels With R

Directions: Write six sentences. Use one word from the Word Box in each sentence.

fur	fork	bird	farm	horn	barn

1. _____

   _____

2. _____

   _____

3. _____

   _____

4. _____

   _____

5. _____

   _____

6. _____

   _____

OI and OY

Directions: Write the word from the Word Box that names each picture.

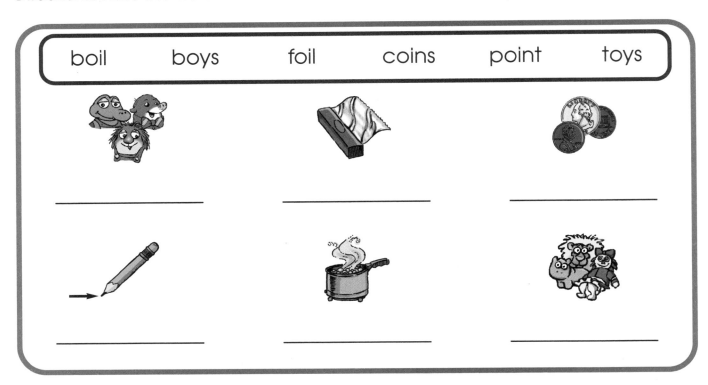

| boil | boys | foil | coins | point | toys |

_____   _____   _____

_____   _____   _____

Directions: Write two sentences. Use one word from above in each sentence.

1. _____

   _____

2. _____

   _____

OI and OY

Directions: Write the missing letters **oi** or **oy** for each word. Then, write the word again.

1. t_____   _____

2. b_____l   _____

3. c_____n   _____

4. b_____s   _____

5. s_____l   _____

6. _____ster   _____

7. _____l   _____

8. f_____l   _____

9. t_____s   _____

10. p_____nt   _____

OI and OY

Directions: Write the word from the Word Box that best completes each sentence.

| boys | voice | enjoys | noise | point |
| soil | join | toys | coins | |

1. Her loud _____ hurts my ears.

2. I broke the _____ on my pencil.

3. How many _____ do you have in your pocket?

4. We gave the baby two new _____ to play with.

5. Our car is making a funny _____.

6. Those _____ are friends from school.

7. Little Critter is going to _____ the reading club.

8. We got the _____ ready so we could plant our garden.

9. Mom _____ going to the library.

Name _____

OU and OW

Directions: Write the word from the Word Box that names each picture.

shower	pound	plow	crown	house	clown
cow	blouse	flower	bounce	frown	gown

_____   _____   _____

_____   _____   _____

_____   _____   _____

_____   _____   _____

OU and OW

Directions: Write the missing letters **ou** or **ow** for each word. Then, write each word again.

1. cl____d _____

2. m____th _____

3. ____l _____

4. cl____n _____

5. p____nd _____

6.  pl____ _____

7. cr____n _____

8. c____ _____

9. fl____er _____

10. h____se _____

Name _____

OU and OW

Directions: Write the word from the Word Box that best completes each sentence.

clouds   mouse   clown   house   crown
blouse   ground   cows   pound

1. The queen wears a gold _Crown_.

2. The little _mouse_ likes to nibble on cheese.

3. Dad uses the hammer to _blouse_ nails.

4. The _clown_ did funny tricks.

5. Mom has a pretty blue _pound_ and skirt.

6. The _cows_ like to munch on grass.

7. There are puffy white _clouds_ in the sky.

8. I dropped my watch on the _grund_.

9. My _house_ is not far from school.

Review: OI, OY, OU, and OW

Directions: Write a word that rhymes with each word below.

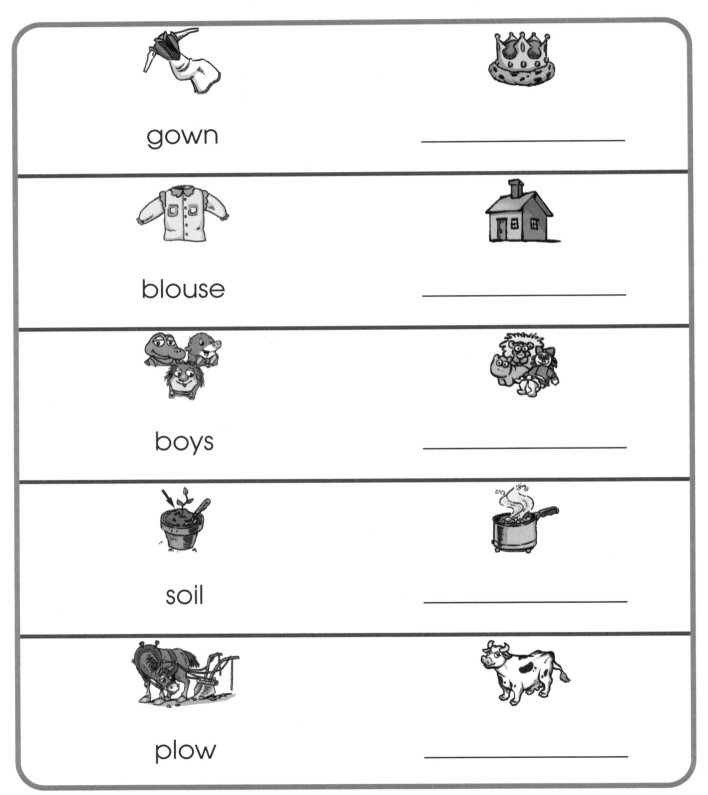

gown   _____

blouse   _____

boys   _____

soil   _____

plow   _____

Check Up: OI, OY, OU, and OW

Directions: Write a word that names each picture. Each word should have the **oi**, **oy**, **ou**, or **ow** vowel pair.

_____   _____   _____

_____   _____   _____

_____   _____   _____

_____   _____   _____

Letters and Their Sounds

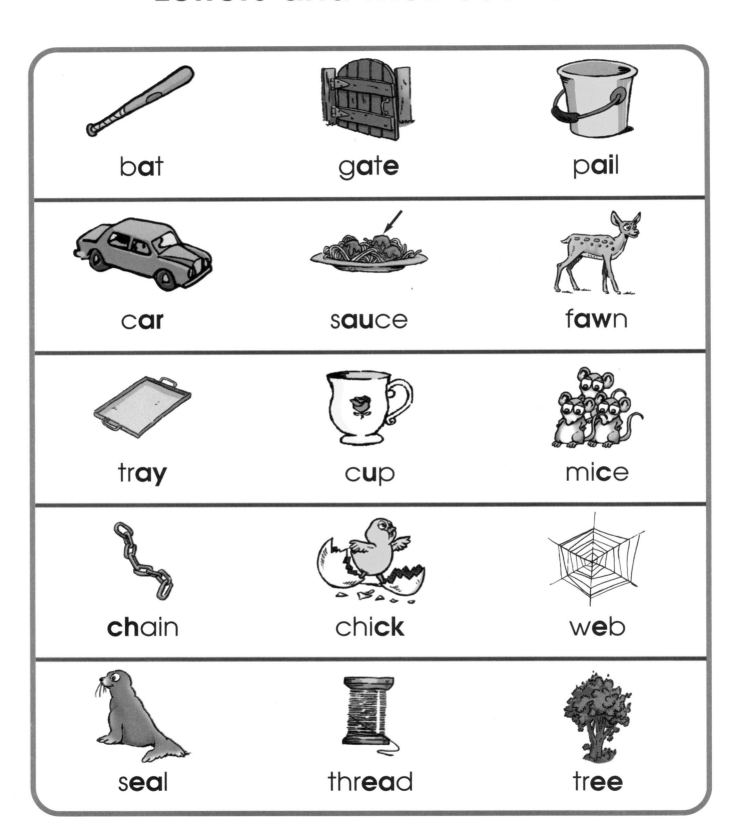

b**a**t

g**a**t**e**

p**ai**l

car

s**au**ce

f**aw**n

tr**ay**

c**u**p

mi**c**e

chain

chi**ck**

w**e**b

seal

thr**ea**d

tr**ee**

Letters and Their Sounds

lett**er**

scr**ew**

game

ca**g**e

hit

fiv**e**

sk**ir**t

knee

wi**ng**

f**ox**

s**oa**p

r**o**se

oil

sp**oo**n

h**oo**k

Letters and Their Sounds

co**rn**

h**ou**se

c**row**

owl

b**oy**s

ship

think

throat

ru**g**

mu**le**

cu**rl**

whale

wrench

sky

pu**ppy**

Practice Page

Practice Page

Practice Page

school

Practice Page

Answer Key

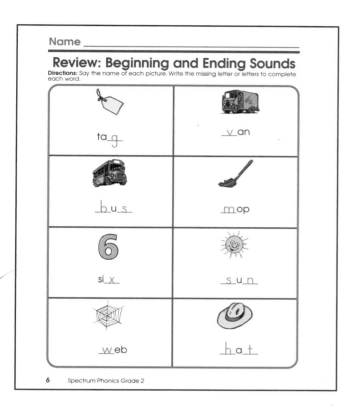

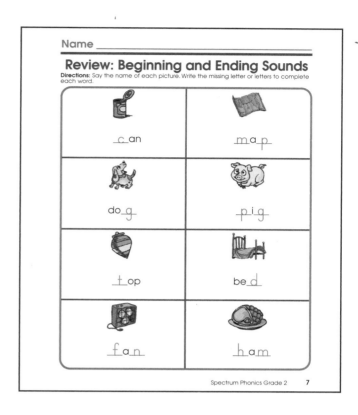

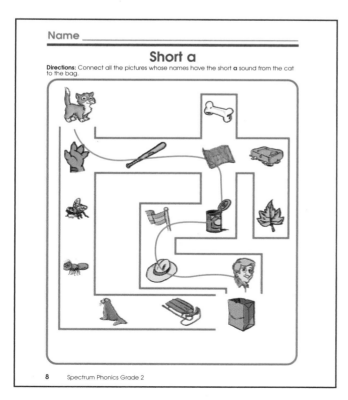

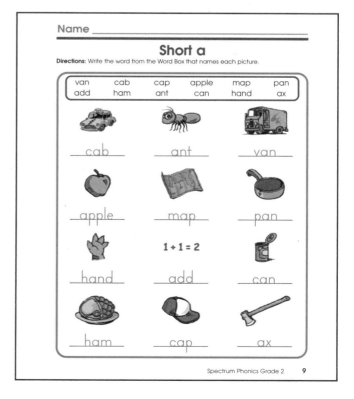

Answer Key

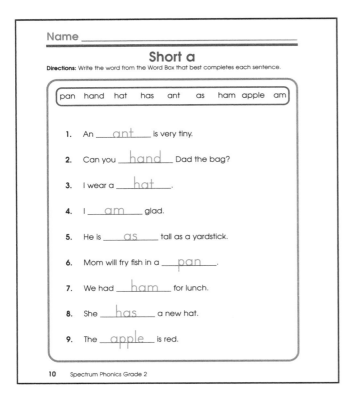

Short a

Directions: Write the word from the Word Box that best completes each sentence.

pan	hand	hat	has	ant	as	ham	apple	am

1. An ___ant___ is very tiny.

2. Can you ___hand___ Dad the bag?

3. I wear a ___hat___ .

4. I ___am___ glad.

5. He is ___as___ tall as a yardstick.

6. Mom will fry fish in a ___pan___ .

7. We had ___ham___ for lunch.

8. She ___has___ a new hat.

9. The ___apple___ is red.

10   Spectrum Phonics Grade 2

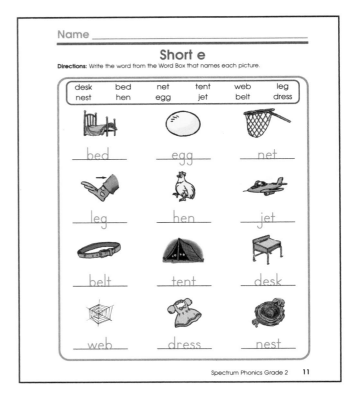

Short e

Directions: Write the word from the Word Box that names each picture.

desk	bed	net	tent	web	leg
nest	hen	egg	jet	belt	dress

bed   egg   net

leg   hen   jet

belt   tent   desk

web   dress   nest

Spectrum Phonics Grade 2   11

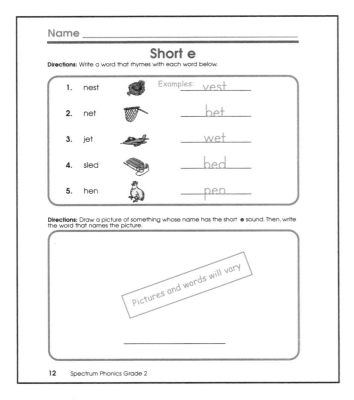

Short e

Directions: Write a word that rhymes with each word below.

Examples: ___vest___

1. nest   ___vest___
2. net   ___bet___
3. jet   ___wet___
4. sled   ___bed___
5. hen   ___pen___

Directions: Draw a picture of something whose name has the short e sound. Then, write the word that names the picture.

Pictures and words will vary

_____

12   Spectrum Phonics Grade 2

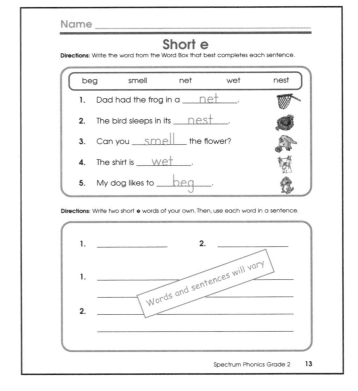

Short e

Directions: Write the word from the Word Box that best completes each sentence.

beg	smell	net	wet	nest

1. Dad had the frog in a ___net___ .
2. The bird sleeps in its ___nest___ .
3. Can you ___smell___ the flower?
4. The shirt is ___wet___ .
5. My dog likes to ___beg___ .

Directions: Write two short e words of your own. Then, use each word in a sentence.

1. _____   2. _____

1. _____

Words and sentences will vary

2. _____

Spectrum Phonics Grade 2   13

Answer Key

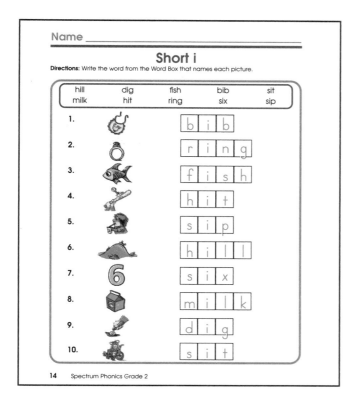

Name _____

Short i

Directions: Write the word from the Word Box that names each picture.

hill	dig	fish	bib	sit
milk	hit	ring	six	sip

1. b i b
2. r i n g
3. f i s h
4. h i t
5. s i p
6. h i l l
7. s i x
8. m i l k
9. d i g
10. s i t

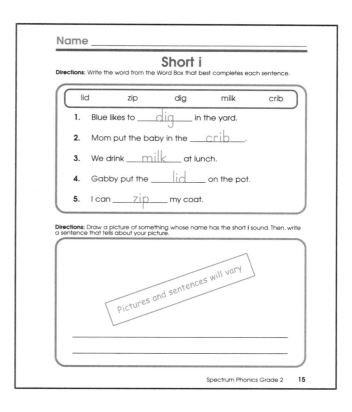

Name _____

Short i

Directions: Write the word from the Word Box that best completes each sentence.

lid	zip	dig	milk	crib

1. Blue likes to ____dig____ in the yard.
2. Mom put the baby in the ____crib____.
3. We drink ____milk____ at lunch.
4. Gabby put the ____lid____ on the pot.
5. I can ____zip____ my coat.

Directions: Draw a picture of something whose name has the short i sound. Then, write a sentence that tells about your picture.

Pictures and sentences will vary

_____

_____

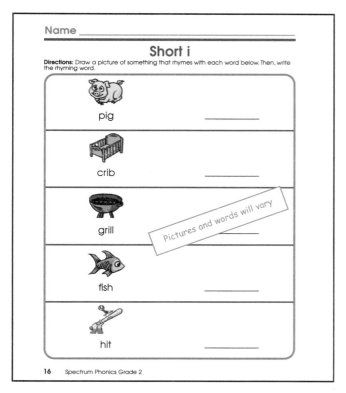

Name _____

Short i

Directions: Draw a picture of something that rhymes with each word below. Then, write the rhyming word.

pig _____

crib _____

grill _____

Pictures and words will vary

fish _____

hit _____

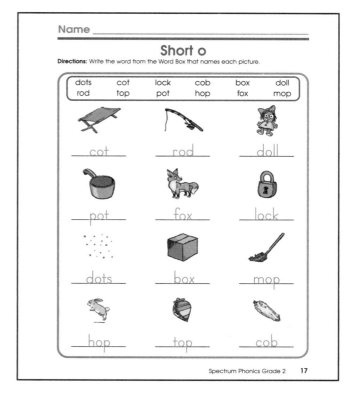

Name _____

Short o

Directions: Write the word from the Word Box that names each picture.

dots	cot	lock	cob	box	doll
rod	top	pot	hop	fox	mop

cot   rod   doll

pot   fox   lock

dots   box   mop

hop   top   cob

Answer Key

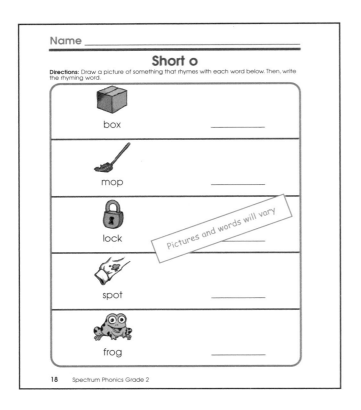

Short o

Directions: Draw a picture of something that rhymes with each word below. Then, write the rhyming word.

box _____

mop _____

lock _____

spot _____

frog _____

Pictures and words will vary

18   Spectrum Phonics Grade 2

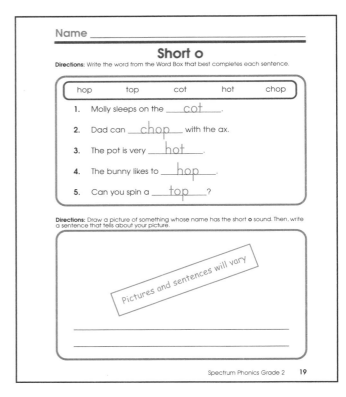

Short o

Directions: Write the word from the Word Box that best completes each sentence.

| hop | top | cot | hot | chop |

1. Molly sleeps on the ___cot___.
2. Dad can ___chop___ with the ax.
3. The pot is very ___hot___.
4. The bunny likes to ___hop___.
5. Can you spin a ___top___?

Directions: Draw a picture of something whose name has the short **o** sound. Then, write a sentence that tells about your picture.

Pictures and sentences will vary

Spectrum Phonics Grade 2   19

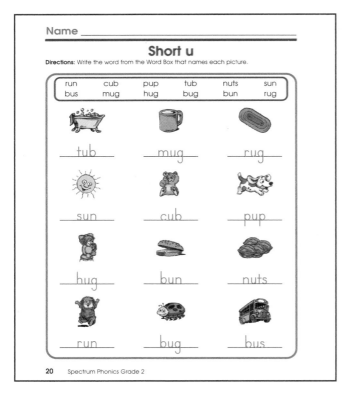

Short u

Directions: Write the word from the Word Box that names each picture.

| run | cub | pup | tub | nuts | sun |
| bus | mug | hug | bug | bun | rug |

tub   mug   rug

sun   cub   pup

hug   bun   nuts

run   bug   bus

20   Spectrum Phonics Grade 2

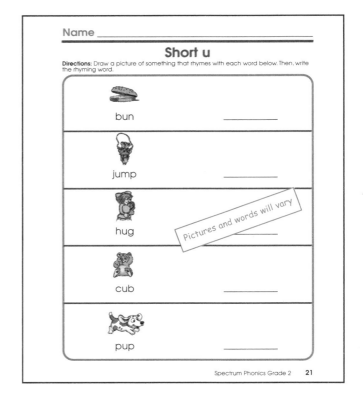

Short u

Directions: Draw a picture of something that rhymes with each word below. Then, write the rhyming word.

bun _____

jump _____

hug _____

cub _____

pup _____

Pictures and words will vary

Spectrum Phonics Grade 2   21

Answer Key

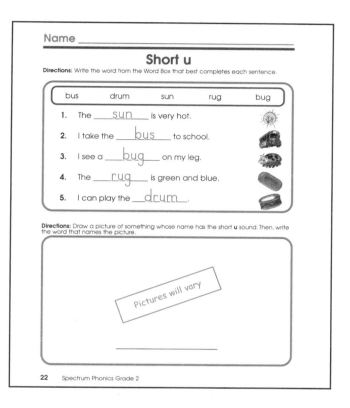

Name _____

Short u

Directions: Write the word from the Word Box that best completes each sentence.

bus	drum	sun	rug	bug

1. The ___sun___ is very hot.
2. I take the ___bus___ to school.
3. I see a ___bug___ on my leg.
4. The ___rug___ is green and blue.
5. I can play the ___drum___.

Directions: Draw a picture of something whose name has the short **u** sound. Then, write the word that names the picture.

Pictures will vary

_____

22   Spectrum Phonics Grade 2

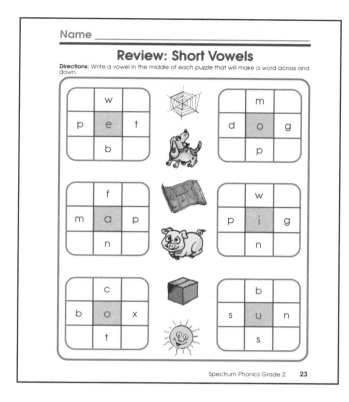

Name _____

Review: Short Vowels

Directions: Write a vowel in the middle of each puzzle that will make a word across and down.

p e t / w e b

d o g / m o p

m a p / f a n

p i g / w i g

b o x / c o t

s u n / b u s

Spectrum Phonics Grade 2   23

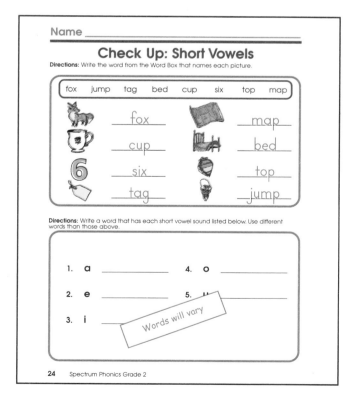

Name _____

Check Up: Short Vowels

Directions: Write the word from the Word Box that names each picture.

fox	jump	tag	bed	cup	six	top	map

fox   map
cup   bed
six   top
tag   jump

Directions: Write a word that has each short vowel sound listed below. Use different words than those above.

1. a _____
2. e _____
3. i _____
4. o _____
5. u _____

Words will vary

24   Spectrum Phonics Grade 2

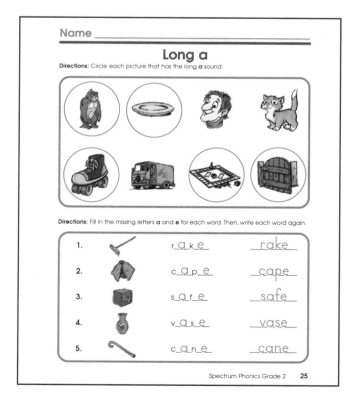

Name _____

Long a

Directions: Circle each picture that has the long **a** sound.

Directions: Fill in the missing letters **a** and **e** for each word. Then, write each word again.

1. r_a_k_e_   rake
2. c_a_p_e_   cape
3. s_a_f_e_   safe
4. v_a_s_e_   vase
5. c_a_n_e_   cane

Spectrum Phonics Grade 2   25

Spectrum Phonics Grade 2   **133**

Answer Key

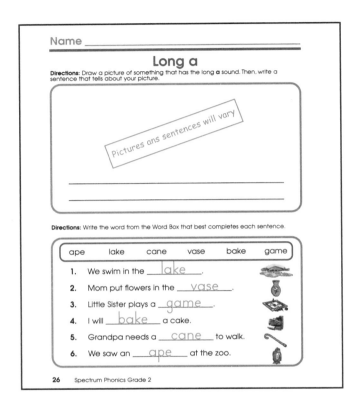

Long a

Directions: Draw a picture of something that has the long **a** sound. Then, write a sentence that tells about your picture.

Pictures ans sentences will vary

Directions: Write the word from the Word Box that best completes each sentence.

ape	lake	cane	vase	bake	game

1. We swim in the __lake__.
2. Mom put flowers in the __vase__.
3. Little Sister plays a __game__.
4. I will __bake__ a cake.
5. Grandpa needs a __cane__ to walk.
6. We saw an __ape__ at the zoo.

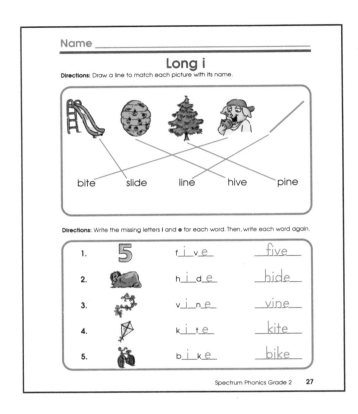

Long i

Directions: Draw a line to match each picture with its name.

bite   slide   line   hive   pine

Directions: Write the missing letters **i** and **e** for each word. Then, write each word again.

1. f_i_v_e_   five
2. h_i_d_e_   hide
3. v_i_n_e_   vine
4. k_i_t_e_   kite
5. b_i_k_e_   bike

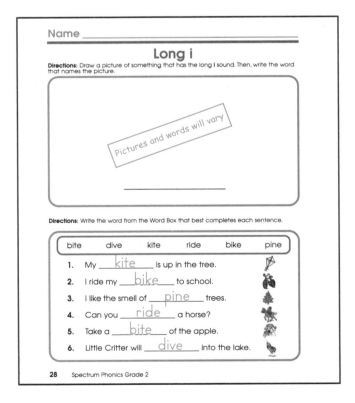

Long i

Directions: Draw a picture of something that has the long **i** sound. Then, write the word that names the picture.

Pictures and words will vary

Directions: Write the word from the Word Box that best completes each sentence.

bite	dive	kite	ride	bike	pine

1. My __kite__ is up in the tree.
2. I ride my __bike__ to school.
3. I like the smell of __pine__ trees.
4. Can you __ride__ a horse?
5. Take a __bite__ of the apple.
6. Little Critter will __dive__ into the lake.

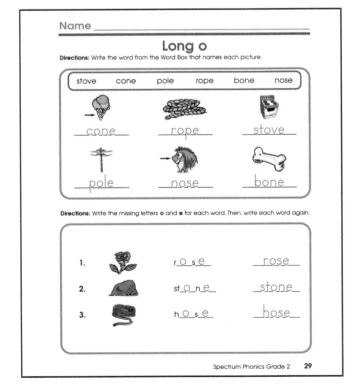

Long o

Directions: Write the word from the Word Box that names each picture.

stove	cone	pole	rope	bone	nose

__cone__   __rope__   __stove__

__pole__   __nose__   __bone__

Directions: Write the missing letters **o** and **e** for each word. Then, write each word again.

1. r_o_s_e_   rose
2. st_o_n_e_   stone
3. h_o_s_e_   hose

Answer Key

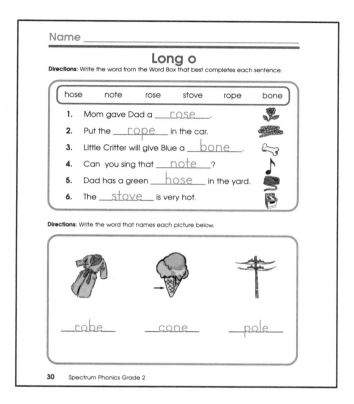

Long o

Directions: Write the word from the Word Box that best completes each sentence.

hose	note	rose	stove	rope	bone

1. Mom gave Dad a __rose__ .
2. Put the __rope__ in the car.
3. Little Critter will give Blue a __bone__ .
4. Can you sing that __note__ ?
5. Dad has a green __hose__ in the yard.
6. The __stove__ is very hot.

Directions: Write the word that names each picture below.

__robe__   __cone__   __pole__

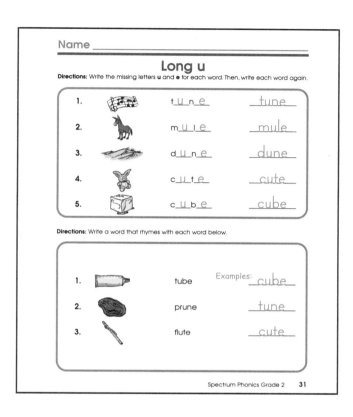

Long u

Directions: Write the missing letters **u** and **e** for each word. Then, write each word again.

1. t u n e   __tune__
2. m u l e   __mule__
3. d u n e   __dune__
4. c u t e   __cute__
5. c u b e   __cube__

Directions: Write a word that rhymes with each word below.

1. tube   Examples: __cube__
2. prune   __tune__
3. flute   __cute__

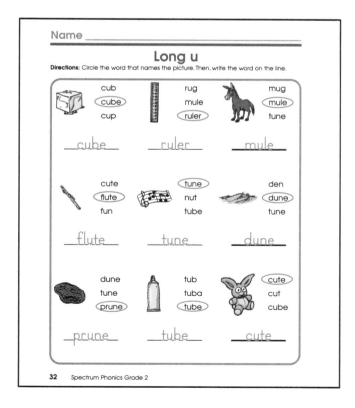

Long u

Directions: Circle the word that names the picture. Then, write the word on the line.

cub / (cube) / cup → __cube__
rug / mule / (ruler) → __ruler__
mug / (mule) / tune → __mule__

cute / (flute) / fun → __flute__
(tune) / nut / tube → __tune__
den / (dune) / tune → __dune__

dune / tune / (prune) → __prune__
tub / tuba / (tube) → __tube__
(cute) / cut / cube → __cute__

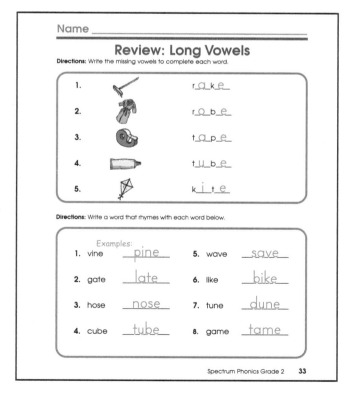

Review: Long Vowels

Directions: Write the missing vowels to complete each word.

1. r a k e
2. r o b e
3. t a p e
4. t u b e
5. k i t e

Directions: Write a word that rhymes with each word below.

Examples:
1. vine __pine__   5. wave __save__
2. gate __late__   6. like __bike__
3. hose __nose__   7. tune __dune__
4. cube __tube__   8. game __tame__

Answer Key

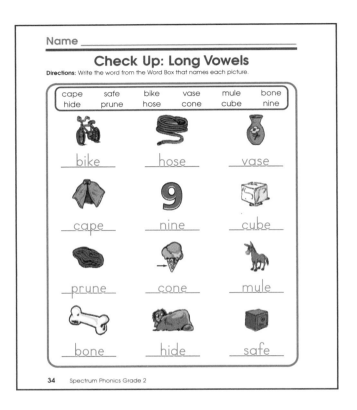

Name _____

Check Up: Long Vowels

Directions: Write the word from the Word Box that names each picture.

cape	safe	bike	vase	mule	bone
hide	prune	hose	cone	cube	nine

bike — hose — vase

cape — nine — cube

prune — cone — mule

bone — hide — safe

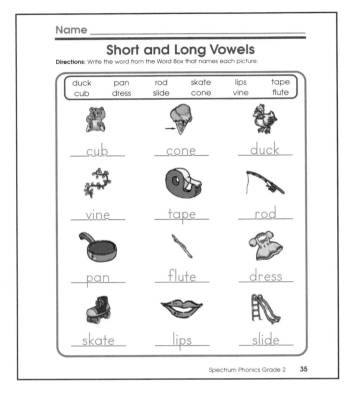

Name _____

Short and Long Vowels

Directions: Write the word from the Word Box that names each picture.

duck	pan	rod	skate	lips	tape
cub	dress	slide	cone	vine	flute

cub — cone — duck

vine — tape — rod

pan — flute — dress

skate — lips — slide

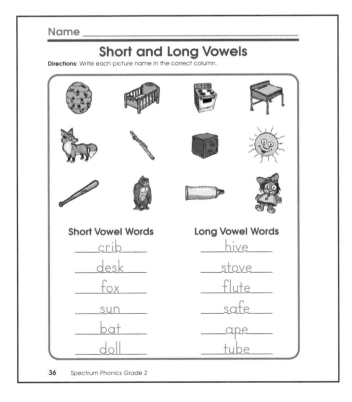

Name _____

Short and Long Vowels

Directions: Write each picture name in the correct column.

Short Vowel Words	Long Vowel Words
crib	hive
desk	stove
fox	flute
sun	safe
bat	ape
doll	tube

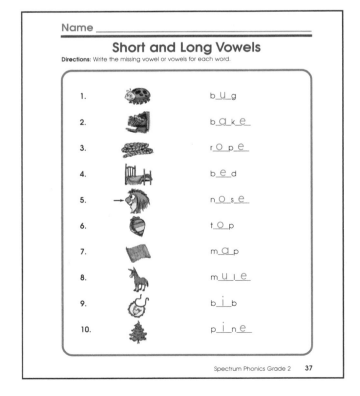

Name _____

Short and Long Vowels

Directions: Write the missing vowel or vowels for each word.

1. b u g
2. b a k e
3. r o p e
4. b e d
5. n o s e
6. t o p
7. m a p
8. m u l e
9. b i b
10. p i n e

Answer Key

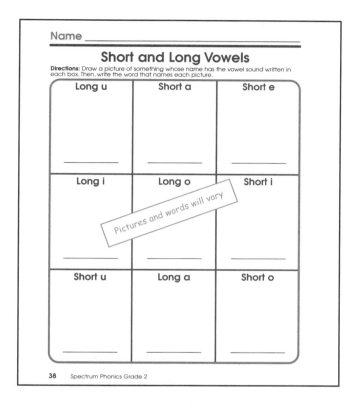

Name _____

Short and Long Vowels

Directions: Draw a picture of something whose name has the vowel sound written in each box. Then, write the word that names each picture.

Long u	Short a	Short e
_____	_____	_____

Long i	Long o	Short i
_____	_____	_____

Pictures and words will vary

Short u	Long a	Short o
_____	_____	_____

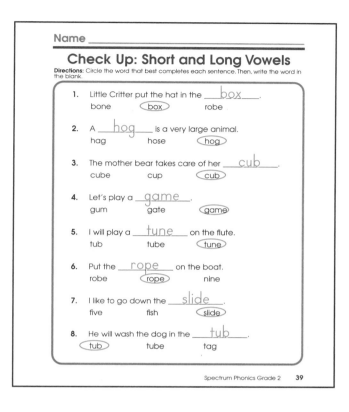

Name _____

Check Up: Short and Long Vowels

Directions: Circle the word that best completes each sentence. Then, write the word in the blank.

1. Little Critter put the hat in the ___box___.
   bone   (box)   robe

2. A ___hog___ is a very large animal.
   hag   hose   (hog)

3. The mother bear takes care of her ___cub___.
   cube   cup   (cub)

4. Let's play a ___game___.
   gum   gate   (game)

5. I will play a ___tune___ on the flute.
   tub   tube   (tune)

6. Put the ___rope___ on the boat.
   robe   (rope)   nine

7. I like to go down the ___slide___.
   five   fish   (slide)

8. He will wash the dog in the ___tub___.
   (tub)   tube   tag

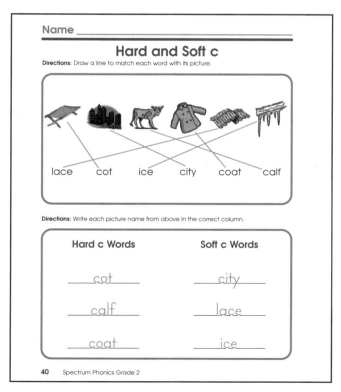

Name _____

Hard and Soft c

Directions: Draw a line to match each word with its picture.

lace   cot   ice   city   coat   calf

Directions: Write each picture name from above in the correct column.

Hard c Words	Soft c Words
cot	city
calf	lace
coat	ice

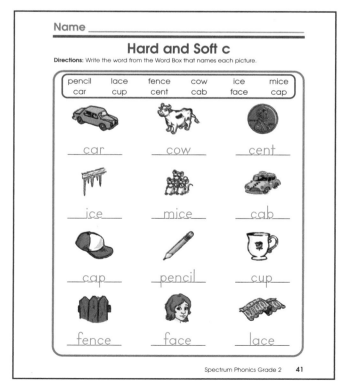

Name _____

Hard and Soft c

Directions: Write the word from the Word Box that names each picture.

pencil	lace	fence	cow	ice	mice
car	cup	cent	cab	face	cap

car   cow   cent

ice   mice   cab

cap   pencil   cup

fence   face   lace

Answer Key

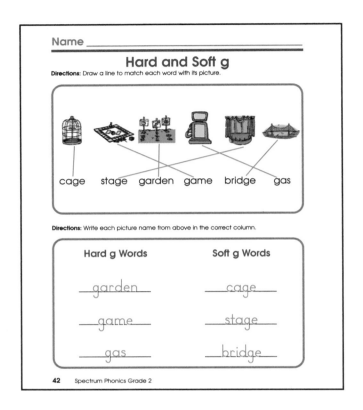

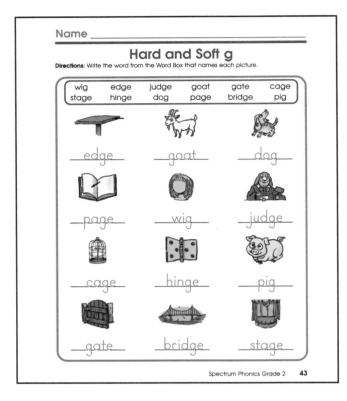

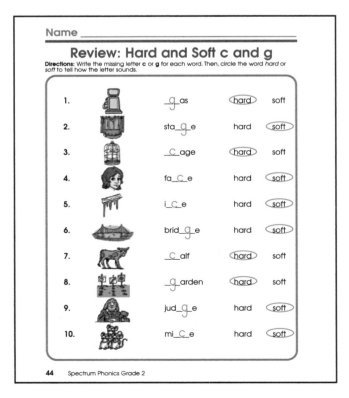

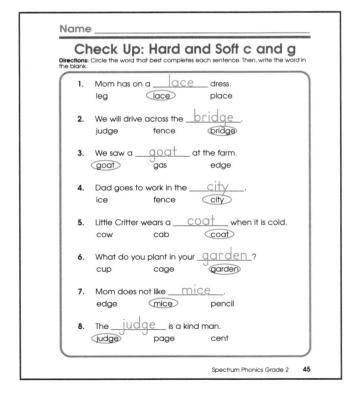

Answer Key

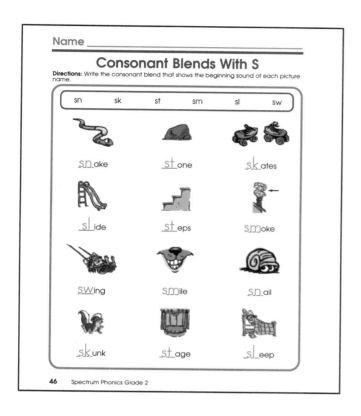

Consonant Blends With S

Directions: Write the consonant blend that shows the beginning sound of each picture name.

sn	sk	st	sm	sl	sw

sn_ake   st_one   sk_ates

sl_ide   st_eps   sm_oke

sw_ing   sm_ile   sn_ail

sk_unk   st_age   sl_eep

46   Spectrum Phonics Grade 2

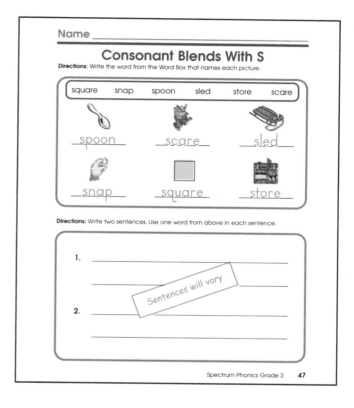

Name

Consonant Blends With S

Directions: Write the word from the Word Box that names each picture.

square	snap	spoon	sled	store	scare

spoon   scare   sled

snap   square   store

Directions: Write two sentences. Use one word from above in each sentence.

1. _____

2. _____

Sentences will vary

Spectrum Phonics Grade 2   47

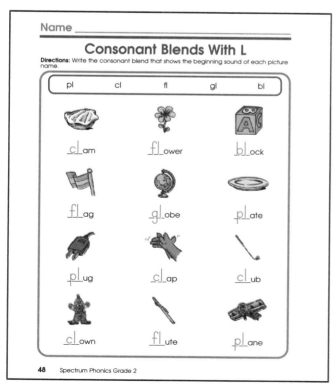

Name

Consonant Blends With L

Directions: Write the consonant blend that shows the beginning sound of each picture name.

pl	cl	fl	gl	bl

cl_am   fl_ower   bl_ock

fl_ag   gl_obe   pl_ate

pl_ug   cl_ap   cl_ub

cl_own   fl_ute   pl_ane

48   Spectrum Phonics Grade 2

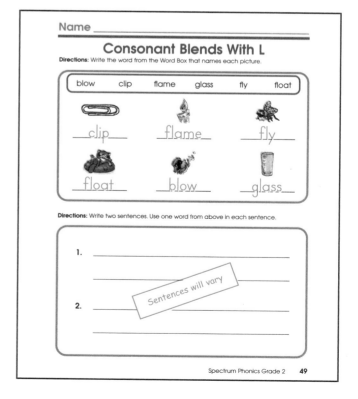

Name

Consonant Blends With L

Directions: Write the word from the Word Box that names each picture.

blow	clip	flame	glass	fly	float

clip   flame   fly

float   blow   glass

Directions: Write two sentences. Use one word from above in each sentence.

1. _____

2. _____

Sentences will vary

Spectrum Phonics Grade 2   49

Answer Key

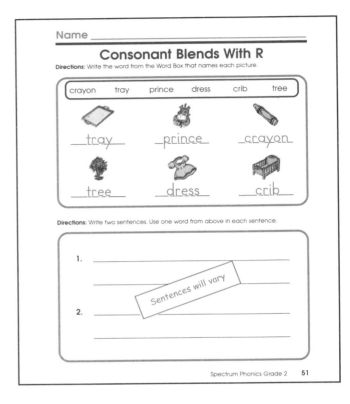

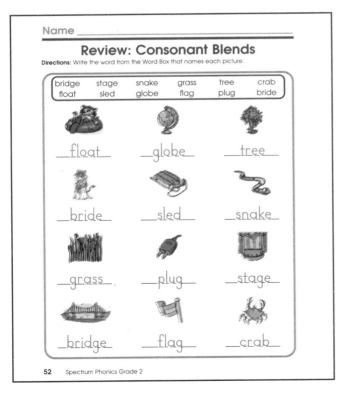

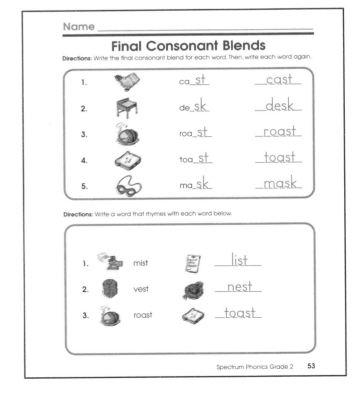

Answer Key

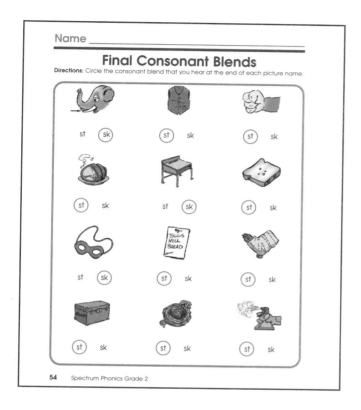

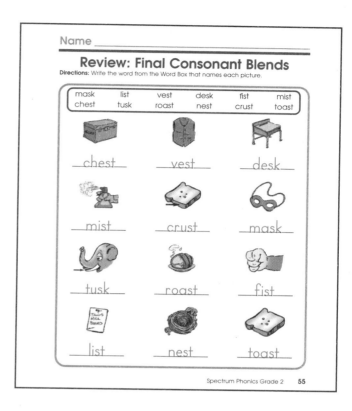

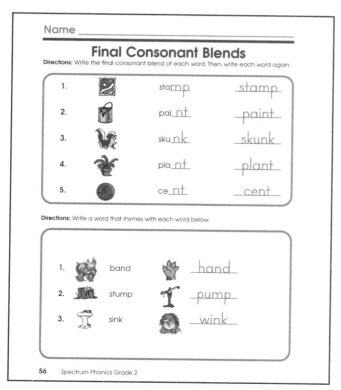

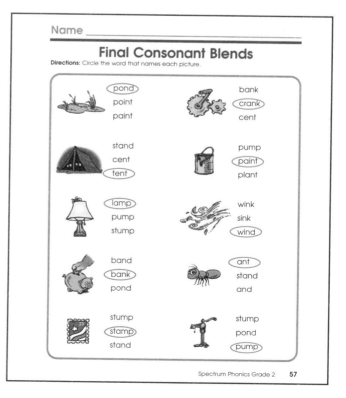

Name ______________________

Final Consonant Blends

Directions: Circle the consonant blend that you hear at the end of each picture name.

st **(sk)**	**(st)** sk	**(st)** sk
(st) sk	st **(sk)**	**(st)** sk
st **(sk)**	**(st)** sk	**(st)** sk
(st) sk	**(st)** sk	**(st)** sk

54 Spectrum Phonics Grade 2

Name ______________________

Review: Final Consonant Blends

Directions: Write the word from the Word Box that names each picture.

mask	list	vest	desk	fist	mist
chest	tusk	roast	nest	crust	toast

chest	vest	desk
mist	crust	mask
tusk	roast	fist
list	nest	toast

Spectrum Phonics Grade 2 55

Name ______________________

Final Consonant Blends

Directions: Write the final consonant blend of each word. Then, write each word again.

1. sta<u>mp</u> stamp
2. pai<u>nt</u> paint
3. sku<u>nk</u> skunk
4. pla<u>nt</u> plant
5. ce<u>nt</u> cent

Directions: Write a word that rhymes with each word below.

1. band hand
2. stump pump
3. sink wink

56 Spectrum Phonics Grade 2

Name ______________________

Final Consonant Blends

Directions: Circle the word that names each picture.

(pond) point paint	bank **(crank)** cent
stand cent **(tent)**	pump **(paint)** plant
(lamp) pump stump	wink sink **(wind)**
band **(bank)** pond	**(ant)** stand and
stump **(stamp)** stand	stump pond **(pump)**

Spectrum Phonics Grade 2 57

Answer Key

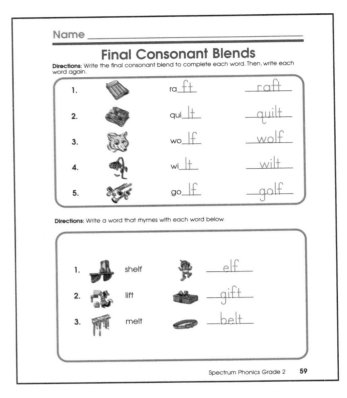

Answer Key

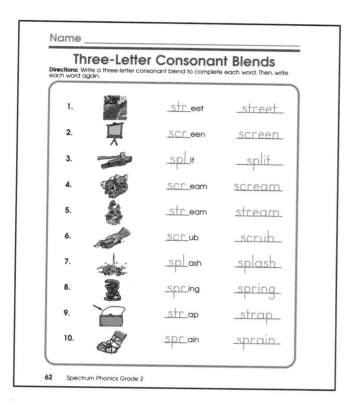

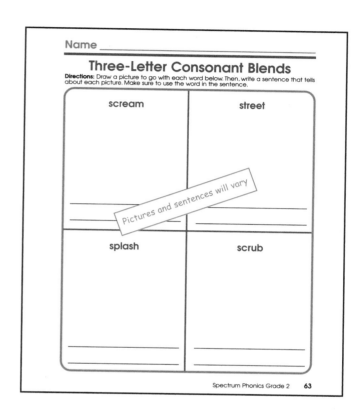

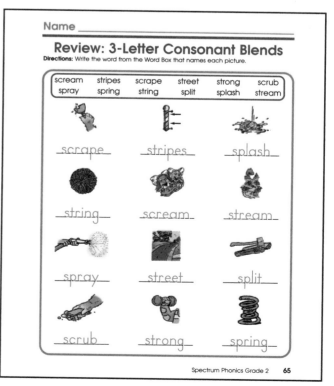

Answer Key

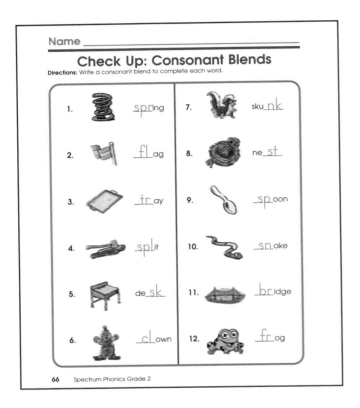

Check Up: Consonant Blends

Directions: Write a consonant blend to complete each word.

1. sp**r**ing
2. **fl**ag
3. **tr**ay
4. **sp**lit
5. de**sk**
6. **cl**own
7. sku**nk**
8. ne**st**
9. **sp**oon
10. **sn**ake
11. **br**idge
12. **fr**og

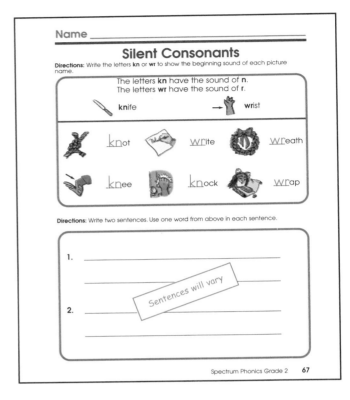

Silent Consonants

Directions: Write the letters **kn** or **wr** to show the beginning sound of each picture name.

The letters **kn** have the sound of **n**.
The letters **wr** have the sound of **r**.

knife → **wr**ist

knot   **wr**ite   **wr**eath
knee   **kn**ock   **wr**ap

Directions: Write two sentences. Use one word from above in each sentence.

1. _____
2. _____

Sentences will vary

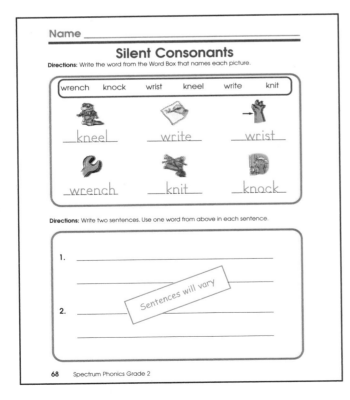

Silent Consonants

Directions: Write the word from the Word Box that names each picture.

wrench	knock	wrist	kneel	write	knit

kneel   write   wrist
wrench   knit   knock

Directions: Write two sentences. Use one word from above in each sentence.

1. _____
2. _____

Sentences will vary

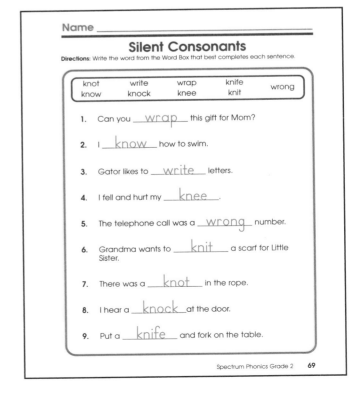

Silent Consonants

Directions: Write the word from the Word Box that best completes each sentence.

knot	write	wrap	knife	
know	knock	knee	knit	wrong

1. Can you **wrap** this gift for Mom?
2. I **know** how to swim.
3. Gator likes to **write** letters.
4. I fell and hurt my **knee**.
5. The telephone call was a **wrong** number.
6. Grandma wants to **knit** a scarf for Little Sister.
7. There was a **knot** in the rope.
8. I hear a **knock** at the door.
9. Put a **knife** and fork on the table.

Answer Key

Name _____

Silent Consonants

Directions: Write the word from the Word Box that names each picture.

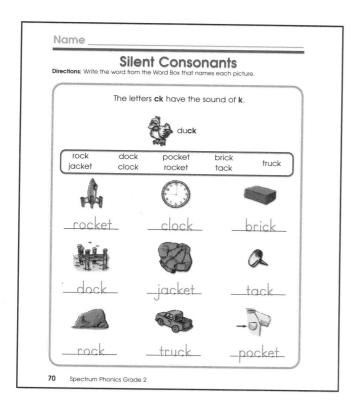

The letters **ck** have the sound of **k**.

du**ck**

rock	dock	pocket	brick	
jacket	clock	rocket	tack	truck

rocket   clock   brick

dock   jacket   tack

rock   truck   pocket

Name _____

Silent Consonants

Directions: Draw a picture to go with each word below. Then, write a sentence that tells about each picture. Make sure to use the word in the sentence.

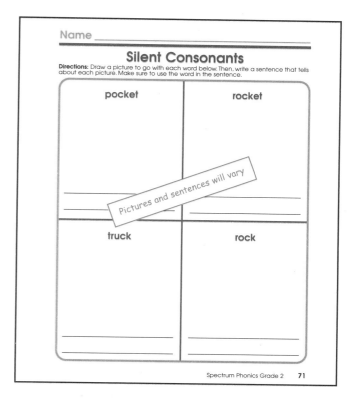

pocket	rocket
truck	rock

Pictures and sentences will vary

Name _____

Silent Consonants

Directions: Write the word from the Word Box that best completes each sentence.

pack	duck	snack	chicks	
clock	tricks	lock	black	dock

1. Did you hear that __duck__ quack?

2. My __clock__ shows the wrong time.

3. Grandma has baby __chicks__ at the farm.

4. Dad gave me a __lock__ for my bike.

5. My dog has __black__ and white fur.

6. Mom steered the boat to the __dock__.

7. Little Critter put his books in his __pack__.

8. Malcolm likes to play __tricks__ on his friends.

9. I am hungry for a __snack__.

Name _____

Silent Consonants

Directions: Write the word from the Word Box that names each picture.

When **g** and **h** are together in a word, they are often silent.

8 ei**gh**t

eighty	light	knight	high	bright	night

knight   80 eighty   high

light   night   bright

Directions: Write two sentences. Use one word from above in each sentence.

1. _____

2. _____

Sentences will vary

Answer Key

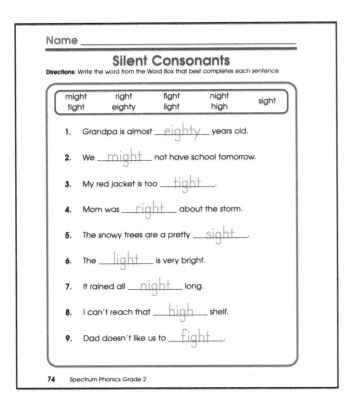

Silent Consonants

Directions: Write the word from the Word Box that best completes each sentence.

might	right	fight	night	sight
tight	eighty	light	high	

1. Grandpa is almost __eighty__ years old.

2. We __might__ not have school tomorrow.

3. My red jacket is too __tight__ .

4. Mom was __right__ about the storm.

5. The snowy trees are a pretty __sight__ .

6. The __light__ is very bright.

7. It rained all __night__ long.

8. I can't reach that __high__ shelf.

9. Dad doesn't like us to __fight__ .

74   Spectrum Phonics Grade 2

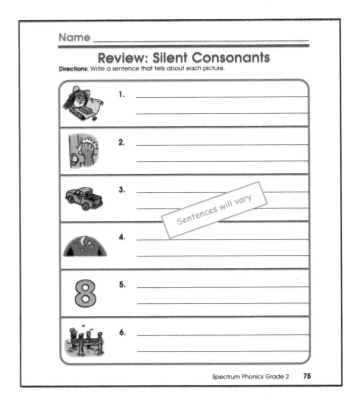

Name

Review: Silent Consonants

Directions: Write a sentence that tells about each picture.

1. _____

2. _____

3. _____

Sentences will vary

4. _____

5. _____

6. _____

Spectrum Phonics Grade 2   75

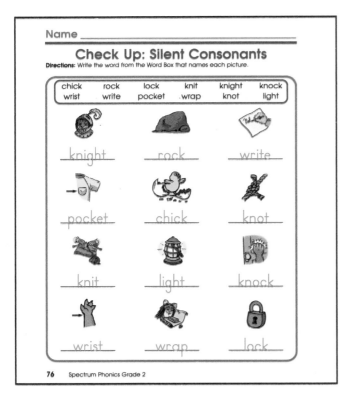

Name

Check Up: Silent Consonants

Directions: Write the word from the Word Box that names each picture.

chick	rock	lock	knit	knight	knock
wrist	write	pocket	wrap	knot	light

knight   rock   write

pocket   chick   knot

knit   light   knock

wrist   wrap   lock

76   Spectrum Phonics Grade 2

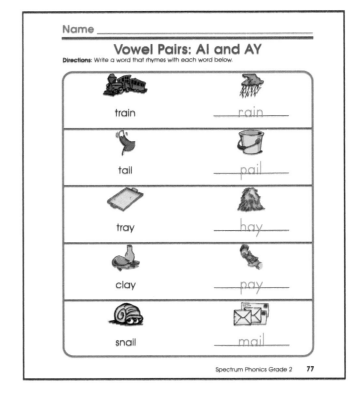

Name

Vowel Pairs: AI and AY

Directions: Write a word that rhymes with each word below.

train   rain

tail   pail

tray   hay

clay   pay

snail   mail

Spectrum Phonics Grade 2   77

Answer Key

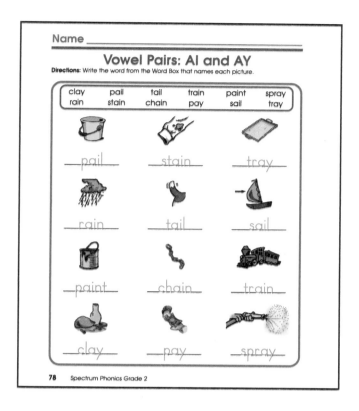

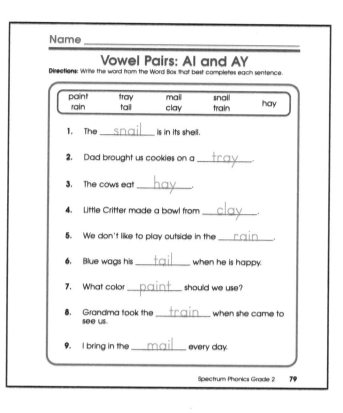

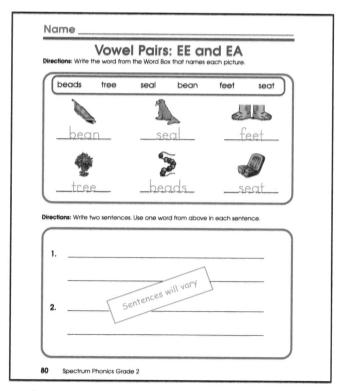

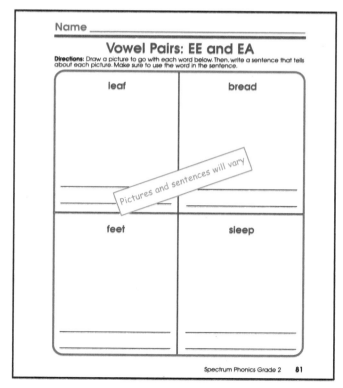

Answer Key

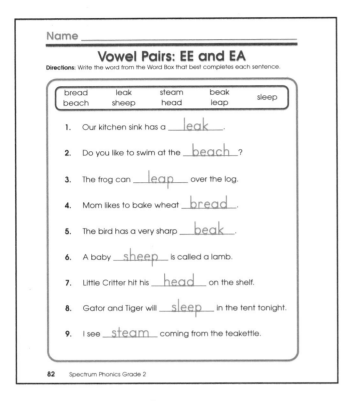

Vowel Pairs: EE and EA

Directions: Write the word from the Word Box that best completes each sentence.

| bread | leak | steam | beak | sleep |
| beach | sheep | head | leap | |

1. Our kitchen sink has a __leak__.
2. Do you like to swim at the __beach__?
3. The frog can __leap__ over the log.
4. Mom likes to bake wheat __bread__.
5. The bird has a very sharp __beak__.
6. A baby __sheep__ is called a lamb.
7. Little Critter hit his __head__ on the shelf.
8. Gator and Tiger will __sleep__ in the tent tonight.
9. I see __steam__ coming from the teakettle.

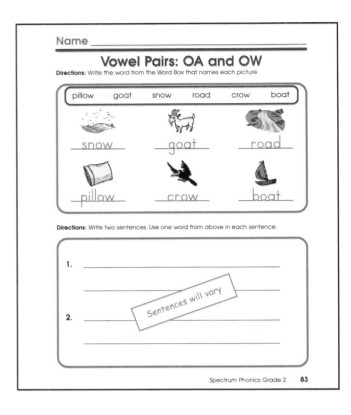

Vowel Pairs: OA and OW

Directions: Write the word from the Word Box that names each picture.

| pillow | goat | snow | road | crow | boat |

__snow__   __goat__   __road__

__pillow__   __crow__   __boat__

Directions: Write two sentences. Use one word from above in each sentence.

1. _____
   Sentences will vary
2. _____

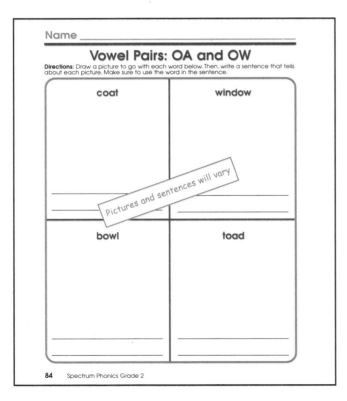

Vowel Pairs: OA and OW

Directions: Draw a picture to go with each word below. Then, write a sentence that tells about each picture. Make sure to use the word in the sentence.

| coat | window |

Pictures and sentences will vary

| bowl | toad |

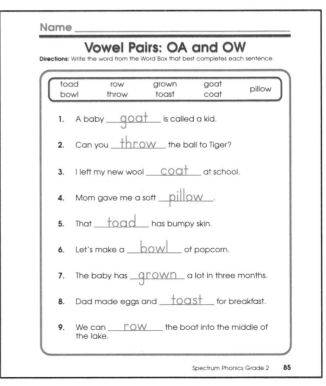

Vowel Pairs: OA and OW

Directions: Write the word from the Word Box that best completes each sentence.

| toad | row | grown | goat | pillow |
| bowl | throw | toast | coat | |

1. A baby __goat__ is called a kid.
2. Can you __throw__ the ball to Tiger?
3. I left my new wool __coat__ at school.
4. Mom gave me a soft __pillow__.
5. That __toad__ has bumpy skin.
6. Let's make a __bowl__ of popcorn.
7. The baby has __grown__ a lot in three months.
8. Dad made eggs and __toast__ for breakfast.
9. We can __row__ the boat into the middle of the lake.

Answer Key

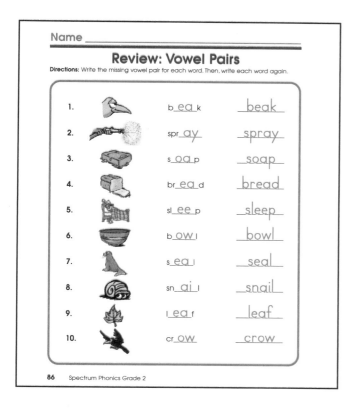

Name _____

Review: Vowel Pairs

Directions: Write the missing vowel pair for each word. Then, write each word again.

1. b_ea_k   beak
2. spr_ay_   spray
3. s_oa_p   soap
4. br_ea_d   bread
5. sl_ee_p   sleep
6. b_ow_l   bowl
7. s_ea_l   seal
8. sn_ai_l   snail
9. l_ea_f   leaf
10. cr_ow_   crow

86   Spectrum Phonics Grade 2

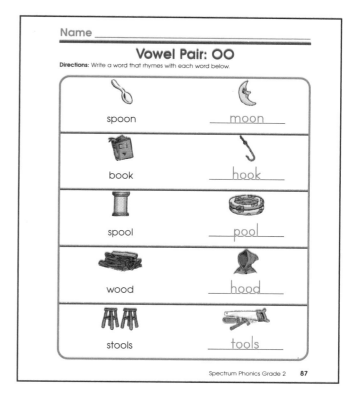

Name _____

Vowel Pair: OO

Directions: Write a word that rhymes with each word below.

spoon	moon
book	hook
spool	pool
wood	hood
stools	tools

Spectrum Phonics Grade 2   87

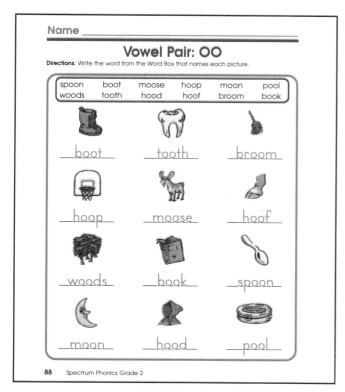

Name _____

Vowel Pair: OO

Directions: Write the word from the Word Box that names each picture.

spoon	boot	moose	hoop	moon	pool
woods	tooth	hood	hoof	broom	book

boot   tooth   broom

hoop   moose   hoof

woods   book   spoon

moon   hood   pool

88   Spectrum Phonics Grade 2

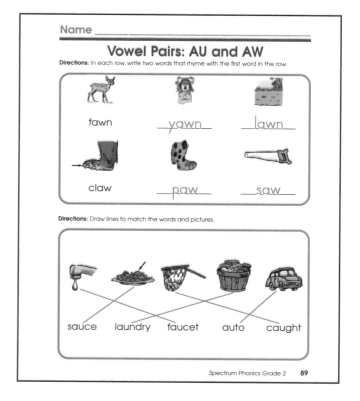

Name _____

Vowel Pairs: AU and AW

Directions: In each row, write two words that rhyme with the first word in the row.

fawn   yawn   lawn

claw   paw   saw

Directions: Draw lines to match the words and pictures.

sauce   laundry   faucet   auto   caught

Spectrum Phonics Grade 2   89

Answer Key

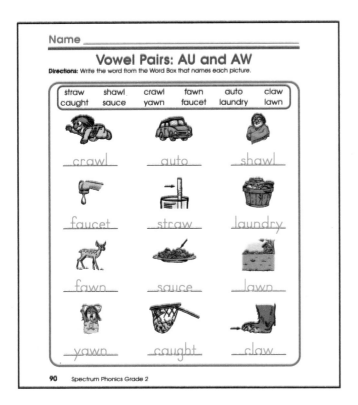

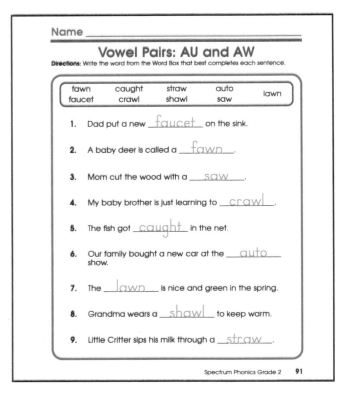

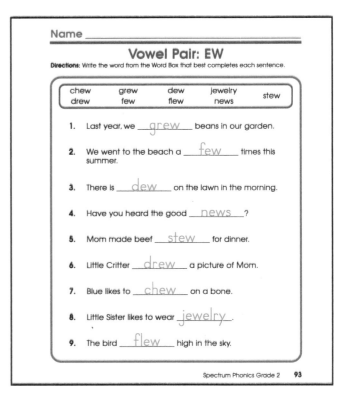

Answer Key

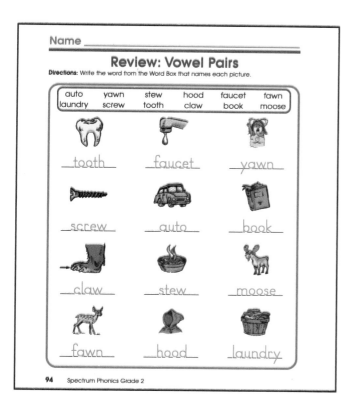

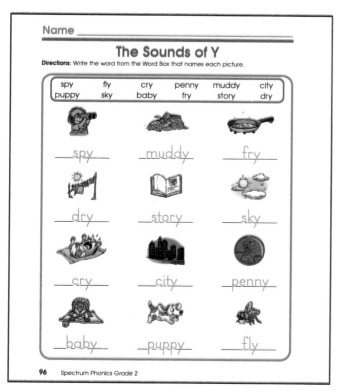

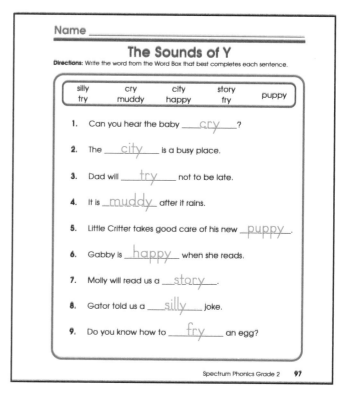

Answer Key

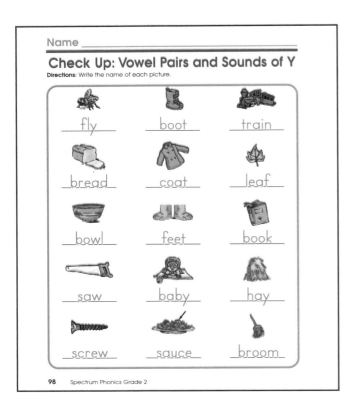

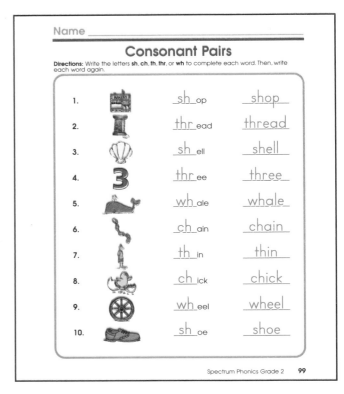

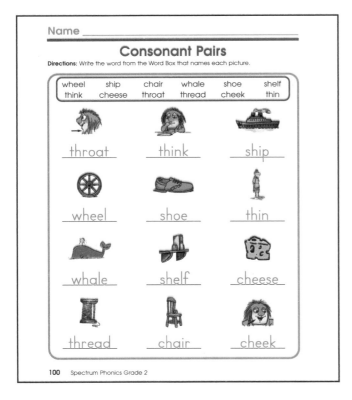

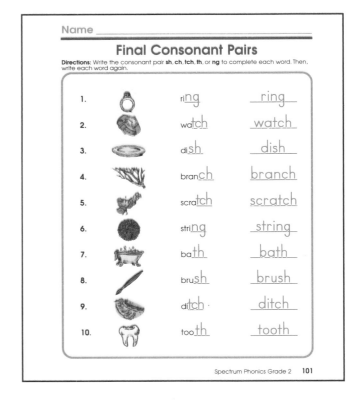

Answer Key

Final Consonant Pairs

Directions: Write a word that rhymes with each word below.

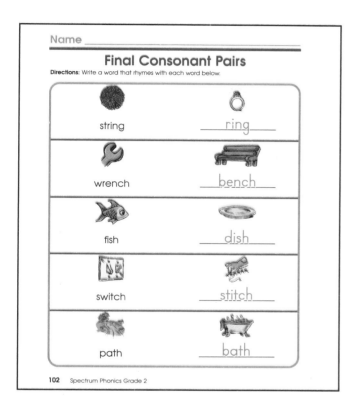

string	ring
wrench	bench
fish	dish
switch	stitch
path	bath

Review: Consonant Pairs

Directions: Write the word from the Word Box that names each picture.

bench	wing	bush	chain	watch	path
three	throne	whale	ship	ring	think

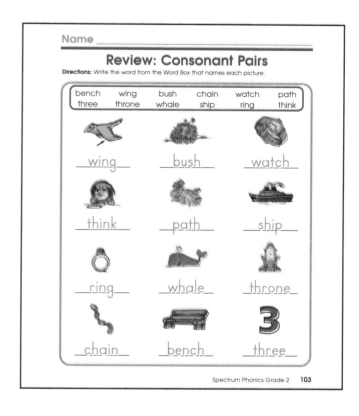

wing   bush   watch

think   path   ship

ring   whale   throne

chain   bench   three

Check Up: Consonant Pairs

Directions: Write the word or words from the Word Box that best completes each sentence.

wing	beach	chunk	bring	bench	cheese
shade	wash	path	ship	splash	shoes

1. The mouse ate a __chunk__ of __cheese__.

2. Mom and Dad sailed on a __ship__.

3. Can you __bring__ a snack to the picnic?

4. Bun Bun walked on the __path__ in the woods.

5. Little Critter is sitting on the green __bench__ in the park.

6. To stay cool, I sit in the __shade__.

7. The bluebird has a broken __wing__.

8. At the __beach__, we like to __splash__ in the water.

9. You should __wash__ your dirty __shoes__.

Vowels With R: AR and ER

Directions: Write the word from the Word Box that names each picture.

jar	barn	yarn	hammer	paper	letter
dart	ladder	slipper	fern	harp	star

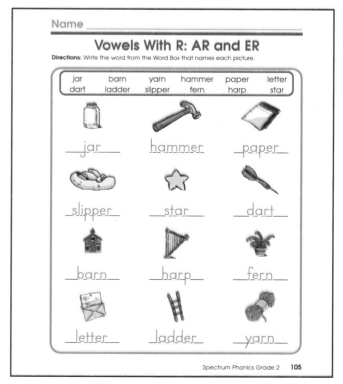

jar   hammer   paper

slipper   star   dart

barn   harp   fern

letter   ladder   yarn

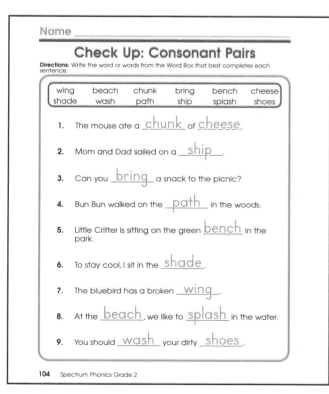

Answer Key

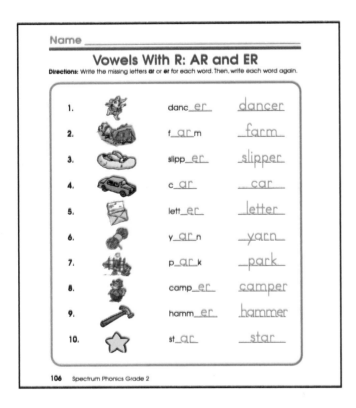

Vowels With R: AR and ER
Directions: Write the missing letters **ar** or **er** for each word. Then, write each word again.

1. danc_er_   dancer
2. f_ar_m   farm
3. slipp_er_   slipper
4. c_ar_   car
5. lett_er_   letter
6. y_ar_n   yarn
7. p_ar_k   park
8. camp_er_   camper
9. hamm_er_   hammer
10. st_ar_   star

106 Spectrum Phonics Grade 2

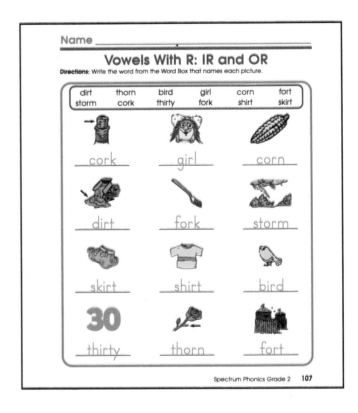

Vowels With R: IR and OR
Directions: Write the word from the Word Box that names each picture.

| dirt | thorn | bird | girl | corn | fort |
| storm | cork | thirty | fork | shirt | skirt |

cork   girl   corn

dirt   fork   storm

skirt   shirt   bird

thirty   thorn   fort

Spectrum Phonics Grade 2 107

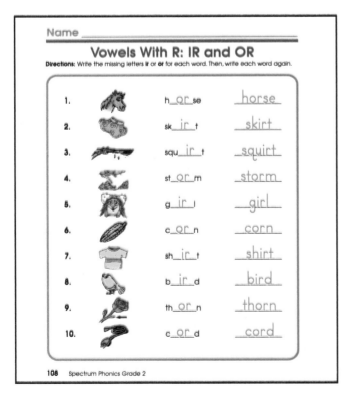

Vowels With R: IR and OR
Directions: Write the missing letters **ir** or **or** for each word. Then, write each word again.

1. h_or_se   horse
2. sk_ir_t   skirt
3. squ_ir_t   squirt
4. st_or_m   storm
5. g_ir_l   girl
6. c_or_n   corn
7. sh_ir_t   shirt
8. b_ir_d   bird
9. th_or_n   thorn
10. c_or_d   cord

108 Spectrum Phonics Grade 2

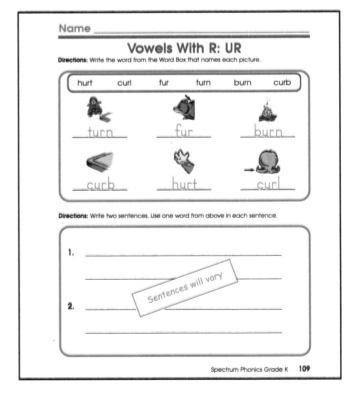

Vowels With R: UR
Directions: Write the word from the Word Box that names each picture.

| hurt | curl | fur | turn | burn | curb |

turn   fur   burn

curb   hurt   curl

Directions: Write two sentences. Use one word from above in each sentence.

1. _____

2. _____

Sentences will vary

Spectrum Phonics Grade K 109

Answer Key

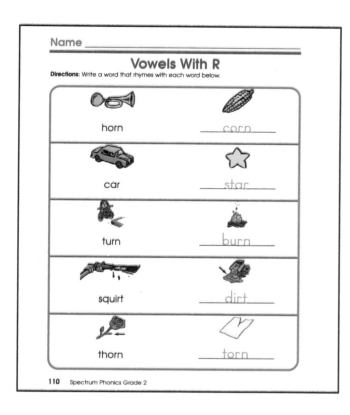

Vowels With R

Directions: Write a word that rhymes with each word below.

horn	corn
car	star
turn	burn
squirt	dirt
thorn	torn

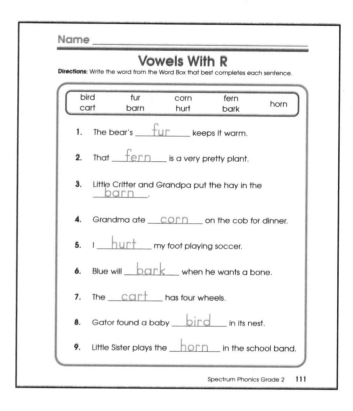

Vowels With R

Directions: Write the word from the Word Box that best completes each sentence.

| bird | fur | corn | fern | |
| cart | barn | hurt | bark | horn |

1. The bear's __fur__ keeps it warm.

2. That __fern__ is a very pretty plant.

3. Little Critter and Grandpa put the hay in the __barn__.

4. Grandma ate __corn__ on the cob for dinner.

5. I __hurt__ my foot playing soccer.

6. Blue will __bark__ when he wants a bone.

7. The __cart__ has four wheels.

8. Gator found a baby __bird__ in its nest.

9. Little Sister plays the __horn__ in the school band.

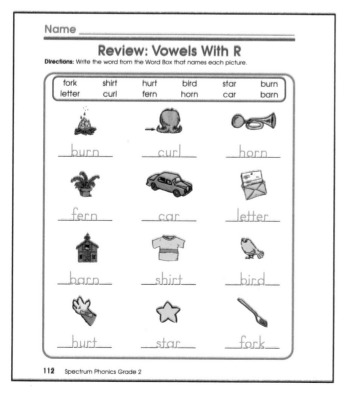

Review: Vowels With R

Directions: Write the word from the Word Box that names each picture.

| fork | shirt | hurt | bird | star | burn |
| letter | curl | fern | horn | car | barn |

burn	curl	horn
fern	car	letter
barn	shirt	bird
hurt	star	fork

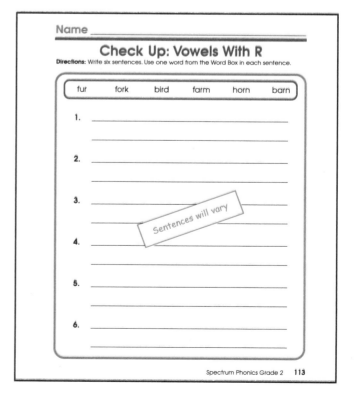

Check Up: Vowels With R

Directions: Write six sentences. Use one word from the Word Box in each sentence.

| fur | fork | bird | farm | horn | barn |

1. _____
2. _____
3. _____
4. _____
5. _____
6. _____

Sentences will vary

Answer Key

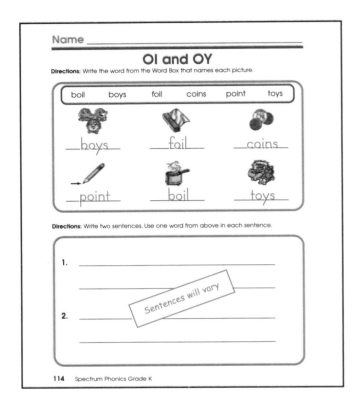

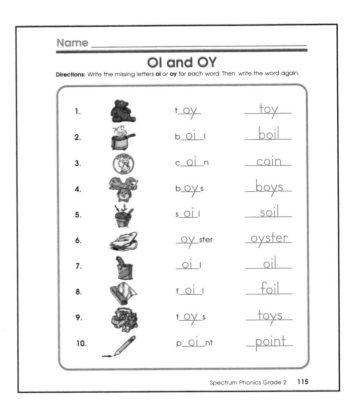

OI and OY

Directions: Write the word from the Word Box that best completes each sentence.

| boys | voice | enjoys | noise | |
| soil | join | toys | coins | point |

1. Her loud __voice__ hurts my ears.

2. I broke the __point__ on my pencil.

3. How many __coins__ do you have in your pocket?

4. We gave the baby two new __toys__ to play with.

5. Our car is making a funny __noise__.

6. Those __boys__ are friends from school.

7. Little Critter is going to __join__ the reading club.

8. We got the __soil__ ready so we could plant our garden.

9. Mom __enjoys__ going to the library.

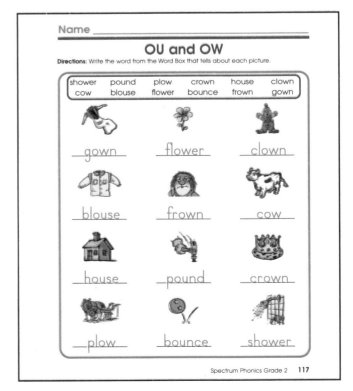

Answer Key

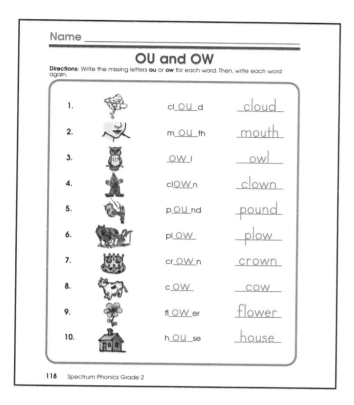

OU and OW

Directions: Write the missing letters **ou** or **ow** for each word. Then, write each word again.

1. cl_ou_d   cloud
2. m_ou_th   mouth
3. _ow_l   owl
4. cl_ow_n   clown
5. p_ou_nd   pound
6. pl_ow_   plow
7. cr_ow_n   crown
8. c_ow_   cow
9. fl_ow_er   flower
10. h_ou_se   house

118   Spectrum Phonics Grade 2

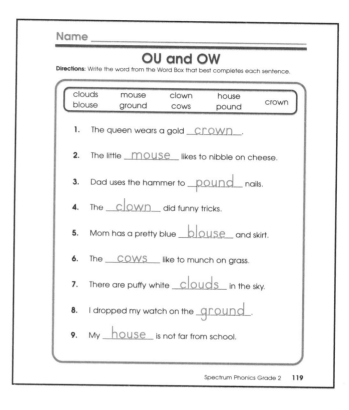

OU and OW

Directions: Write the word from the Word Box that best completes each sentence.

clouds	mouse	clown	house	crown
blouse	ground	cows	pound	

1. The queen wears a gold __crown__.
2. The little __mouse__ likes to nibble on cheese.
3. Dad uses the hammer to __pound__ nails.
4. The __clown__ did funny tricks.
5. Mom has a pretty blue __blouse__ and skirt.
6. The __cows__ like to munch on grass.
7. There are puffy white __clouds__ in the sky.
8. I dropped my watch on the __ground__.
9. My __house__ is not far from school.

Spectrum Phonics Grade 2   119

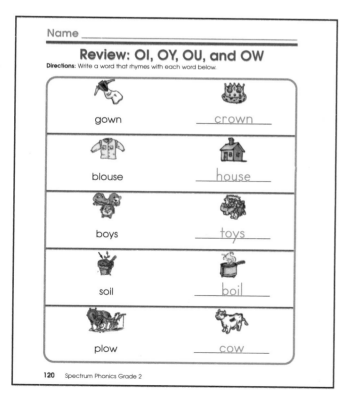

Review: OI, OY, OU, and OW

Directions: Write a word that rhymes with each word below.

gown	crown
blouse	house
boys	toys
soil	boil
plow	cow

120   Spectrum Phonics Grade 2

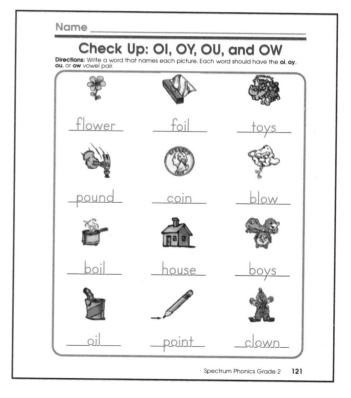

Check Up: OI, OY, OU, and OW

Directions: Write a word that names each picture. Each word should have the **oi, oy, ou,** or **ow** vowel pair.

flower   foil   toys

pound   coin   blow

boil   house   boys

oil   point   clown

Spectrum Phonics Grade 2   121

Notes